PRAISE FOR JON M. SWEENEY'S BOOKS...

"In Sweeney's hands, the story of a man often dismissed as naïve and incompetent becomes an engaging mystery and an enjoyable primer on the ecclesiastical wheeling and dealing of the late Middle Ages."
—Paul Moses, *America* magazine

"Sweeney achieves a fine balance between excellent scholarship and sweet accessibility for every average reader."
—Walter Wangerin, Jr., author of *St. Julian* and *The Book of God*

"Sweeney, in very accessible concepts and language, presents a marvelously contemporary and inclusive theology of sanctity and saints."
—*Catholic Library World*

"A rich resource of information, insights and beauty. . . . Both critical and reverential."
—Bishop Frederick Borsch,
Professor of New Testament and Chair of Anglican Studies, Lutheran Theological Seminary

"Sweeney examines his story and its meaning with un-usual humility. His tone is thankful and affirming, meant to shore up bridges rather than burn them down."
—Betty Smartt Carter, *Books & Culture*

"Jon Sweeney is a fine, informative writer. He has a way of discussing a variety of religious matters in clear, common sense terms. . . . Highly recommended."
—*Church and Synagogue Library Association*

FRANCIS
AND
CLARE

The Holy Conversation of Saints Francis and Clare

FRANCIS
AND
CLARE

A True Story

Jon M. Sweeney

PARACLETE PRESS
BREWSTER, MASSACHUSETTS

2013 First Printing This Edition
2007 First Printing Original Edition

Francis and Clare: A True Story

Copyright © 2007 by Jon M. Sweeney

ISBN: 978-1-61261-454-0

The Library of Congress has catalogued the first edition of this book as follows:
Sweeney, Jon M., 1967-
   Light in the dark ages : the friendship of Francis and Clare of Assisi / by Jon M. Sweeney.
      p. cm.
   Includes bibliographical references and index.
   ISBN 978-1-55725-476-4
   1. Francis, of Assisi, Saint, 1182-1226. 2. Clare, of Assisi, Saint, 1194-1253.
   3. Christian saints--Italy--Assisi--Biography. I. Title.
   BX4700.F6S93 2007
   271'.302--dc22
   [B]   2007007060

10 9 8 7 6 5 4 3 2 1

Published by Paraclete Press
Brewster, Massachusetts
www.paracletepress.com
Printed in the United States of America

FOR CHRISTINA

with respect and affection

OTHER BOOKS BY JON M. SWEENEY

The Road to Assisi (edited)

The St. Francis Prayer Book

The St. Clare Prayer Book

The Little Flowers of Saint Francis (edited and translated)

Francis of Assisi in His Own Words (edited and translated)

LIST OF ILLUSTRATIONS

"The Holy Conversation of Saints Francis and Clare,"
contemporary icon by Marek Czarnecki, reproduced in black and white
. . . frontispiece

All of the other illustrations are reproductions of Giotto,
or School of Giotto, frescoes from Assisi, Padua, and Florence.

CONTENTS

FRANCIS
AND
CLARE

BEGINNINGS

Wrapped in the colorful silks imported and sold by Peter Bernardone, most of the highborn girls in Assisi paid close attention to matters of courtship, honor, and family. Seasonal events in the cathedral church and the governor's estate occupied their minds, and their hearts were wooed by the songs of young would-be troubadours carousing in the streets below their bedroom windows after dark. Francis Bernardone was once one of those young men. But by all accounts, Clare Favorone was never one of those girls.

Francis and Clare were both children of Assisi, Italy, where being baptized into the Church was once the equivalent of citizenship. They came from what we would call upper-middle-class families. Clare was a young teenager when Francis began his slow process of conversion. She was about fifteen and he was twenty-seven when she first heard him preach about poverty and joy at the San Rufinus cathedral. Her family home bordered the great church, and she was accustomed to regularly attending services there. Hearing Francis preach probably stirred the beginnings of conversion. Feeling God's presence wouldn't have frightened her, for she was never easily frightened. Only two years later, Clare began her own rejection of vanity, self-interest, and wealth. She quietly renounced worldly affairs in March 1212 and became the first woman to join Francis and his friars. These were simple gestures, but they were nevertheless recognized by Clare's contemporaries as the first marks of an independent woman.

The life of Francis is well-known, but Clare's less so. Her first biographer tells us that she secretly wore hair shirts—rough garments of asceticism and penance—from an early age, and while we may not take such a description as absolute fact, the point is that Clare was different.[1] She didn't pine for the latest fabrics and dyes that Peter Bernardone brought back with him from his trips to France. She wasn't looking anxiously for her future husband or counting the days until her wedding. From an early age, she seemed to others to be out of step with the expectations of a fortunate girl from a promising family.

Within four and one-half years of Clare's conversion, we have evidence from a letter written by Jacques of Vitry, who was elected the bishop of Acre in 1216 and traveled to Perugia upon the death of Pope Innocent III, that there were many vibrant communities of friars and sisters throughout Italy. Disappointed with the heresy and worldliness that he discovered during his travels in Italy, the Frenchman described the early Franciscans this way, as he discovered them for the first time:

> Many well-to-do secular people of both sexes, having left all things for Christ, had fled the world. They were called "Lesser Brothers" and "Lesser Sisters". . . . They are in no way occupied with temporal things, but with fervent desire and ardent zeal they labor each day to draw from the vanities

of the world souls that are perishing, and draw them to their way of life. Thanks be to God, they have already reaped great fruit and have converted many. Those who have heard them, say: "Come," so that one group brings another. . . . During the day they go into the cities and villages giving themselves over to the active life in order to gain others; at night, however, they return to their hermitage or solitary places to devote themselves to contemplation.[2]

And so it was. The Franciscan movement began in simple ways, with bold but modest intentions, and grew rapidly. The Franciscans presumed to live like Jesus. Francis, Clare, and their early followers were part of a select group of Christians through the ages who have been passionately spiritual and ardently practical at the same time. In the long history of faith, spiritual vitality has flowed best when humans have rediscovered Jesus and tried to replicate his life in their own. Moral and practical decisions have been infused with spiritual vitality in those eras when the words of Jesus were followed most closely.

The Franciscans' worldview praised beauty and ethics both. They were of one spirit with the first Christian churches in Rome and Asia Minor, the Desert Fathers and Mothers of late antiquity, the first followers of St. Benedict at medieval Subiaco, reform-minded Carmelites under St. Teresa of Avila and St. John of the Cross, and others who have imitated the life and emulated the teachings of Jesus. Through their partnership, Francis and Clare brought light into the darkness of the late Middle Ages.

In the words of Dante, Francis was the "Morning Star" or Sun that rises from the East to shine new light upon the dawn. His life was full of poetry—both lived and spoken. His greatest biographer, Paul Sabatier, goes so far as to describe the impact of Francis on his era this way: "[His life] closed the reign of Byzantine art and of the thought of which it was the image. It is the end of dogmatism and authority. Uncertainty became permissible in some small measure. It marks a date in the history of the human conscience."[3]

This book is a chronicle of the spirit that animated Francis and Clare. Through their joy-filled and sometimes foolish lives of poverty and charity, both Europe and the Christian faith changed. The darkness of the medieval worldview was enlightened in ways that would lead to reformations of religious thought, poetry, and song, a renaissance of realism in art, Scriptures in local languages, ways of practicing faith outside of church, and new understandings of God and the world. For at least a generation, Francis and Clare and the first Franciscans changed the heart of faith. And since their time, they have inspired millions of us who desire to capture something of their spirit.

At the same time, there is an undeniable sadness attached to this story. The movement that Francis began in 1209 and that Clare continued after his death and until her own passing in 1253 was fraught with conflict and dissention. The original ideals that inspired so many early followers began to fade away within two decades. We will explore all of these themes in the chapters below.

Each chapter begins by telling one of the key stories of the early Franciscan experience and then explores issues and themes from their spirituality. The chapters are organized in roughly chronological order. For example, chapter 3 describes the stages of Francis's conversion and also introduces the concept of living in voluntary poverty. Chapter 4 opens with the story of how Francis first heard the voice of God and discusses the corruption of the thirteenth-century Church. Chapter 5 tells of the beginning of the Franciscan movement while exploring foolishness and joy—two key aspects of the personality of Franciscan spirituality—and the stormy relationship between Francis and Clare and their parents. Chapter 6 describes Clare's conversion and discusses what it means to imitate Christ. And so on. Each of the sixteen chapters raises questions that explore the spirituality of Francis and Clare, the origins of their movement, and how beliefs and practices from eight hundred years ago relate to what we do today.

It will become obvious throughout *Light in the Dark Ages* that I admire the saints from Assisi and that I believe we should model ourselves after them. However, this book is not without criticism of their ideals and practices, particularly in chapters 5, 6, and 8. Whether you are reading this while sitting at home, on retreat, on pilgrimage, or as part of a group study, each chapter will point you in new directions. The stories and issues traced throughout the book form a basic outline of the early movement and in the process show their relevance, as well as their incongruities, with our lives today. That is, after all, the point of my writing and your reading these pages: we seek to not only understand who Francis and Clare were, but also how to live in the spirit of their ideals today.

In 1986, Pope John Paul II coined the term "the spirit of Assisi," expressing what millions of people have felt since the deaths of Francis and Clare. Assisi certainly holds memories and stories of a time not to be forgotten, but more important, there is a vitality to the early Franciscan way of life that still draws people in our time. This doesn't mean that we necessarily aim to become professed religious, joining one modern Franciscan order or another. But for millions of people today, those little flowers of faith are not saccharine monikers, but rather instances of what can happen to sweeten up any human life, as well as the community of those around it.

THE SOURCES FOR OUR STORY

I should say a few words about the sources used for understanding the lives of Francis and Clare. Controversy surrounds the ways in which their lives are interpreted, and these controversies wind all the way back to the first days after Francis's death. There were many early attempts to tell the story of his life, and sometimes the interpretations clash.

Most important among all of the early biographies are those written by Thomas of Celano and Bonaventure. Thomas was a contemporary of Francis who joined the Order in 1215, while Bonaventure was a second-generation Franciscan who never knew the founder. Thomas of Celano wrote the first two lives of Francis and the first biography of Clare. For that reason, Thomas is enormously important for understanding the relationship between them. In the case of both Francis and Clare, Thomas's biographies are the closest we have to understanding their lives and experiences.[4] Throughout the present work, I will refer to Thomas's two biographies of Francis as *First Life* and *Second Life*, for clarity and simplicity's sake.

It was about twenty-five years after Thomas's *First Life* was published that Bonaventure—who was then the minister-general of the Franciscan Order—authored his revision. Most of Bonaventure's book came straight from the stories of Thomas of Celano, but he reinterpreted them for a new generation. Three years after writing, Bonaventure declared his to be the only *authorized* biography, and copies of Thomas's two earlier books were ordered destroyed. This is an early sign of how the Franciscans, not even one generation removed from their founder, sought to control the interpretation of his life. We will discuss this more in detail below.

Uncovering the real Francis beneath layers of legend has been the vocation of many great scholars of the last 120 years. Chief among them is Paul Sabatier, who wrote the first modern biography of Francis in 1894.[5] At the time of Sabatier's writing, the *Fioretti*, or "Little Flowers," was well known. *The Little Flowers of St. Francis* is a collection of tales that were told and retold by the generation of friars who lived after Francis's death. These tales were the spiritual treasure of those men and women who valued the original ideals of Francis most of all. They believed that Thomas of Celano's two biographies of Francis were more faithful to the true intent of their founder than was Bonaventure's. *The Little Flowers* contained fifty-three tales in its original, vernacular, Tuscan compilation—the language that Dante and Boccaccio would soon use for their own epic stories.

Two other important texts had not yet been discovered by the end of the nineteenth century: *The Legend of Perugia* (written around 1312; first published in 1922) and *The Mirror of Perfection* (written around 1318; first published in 1898). These collections of tales have intrigued historians, offering further evidence that the official interpretations of Francis's life are not always the most accurate ones. The picture painted of Francis in these collections is different from the common portrait of him, emphasizing his earthiness, combativeness, foolishness, insistence, and occasionally his quixotic way of communicating with others.

The Mirror of Perfection was so named because it was said by its authors to be "the Mirror of Perfection of a brother Minor; to wit, of the Blessed Francis, wherein we may most sufficiently behold as in a glass the perfection of his calling and profession."[6] Sabatier himself first published *The Mirror* in 1898, controversially claiming in the book's subtitle that it was a firsthand documentation of the life of St. Francis written in 1228 by Francis's close friend and confidante, Brother Leo.[7] If it had indeed been written so early, it would predate even Thomas of Celano's accounts. But in the twenty or so years after Sabatier made this claim, evidence surfaced that suggested a date of composition about ninety years later than Sabatier had hoped. This later evidence ultimately became irrefutable. As often happened throughout the Middle Ages, it was a copyist's error that led to Sabatier's mistake about the priority of *The Mirror*. Before the age of printing, texts were copied by hand, allowing mistakes of content to enter in. In this case, the mistake was in the dating of it. The copyist miscopied one of the Roman numerals, changing it from MCCCXVIII (1318) to MCCXXVIII (1228).

To this day, no one doubts that the essence of this great collection of stories comes from the friars who were closest to Francis: Angelo, Rufinus, and Leo. There is something undeniably fresh, immediate, unpolished, and argumentative about the tales in *The Mirror of Perfection*. Most of the stories are repeated from Thomas of Celano's *Second Life*, but the original wording (of Leo?) is sometimes altered. Together, *Second Life* and *The Mirror* represent the companions of Francis who believed that the leaders of the Order had turned their backs on the true Franciscan ideals. Absolute poverty and humility were being replaced by property and learning. Leo and his companions were called the Spirituals, or friars of the strict observance. As the scholar John Moorman says, "Sabatier was wrong in dating [*The Mirror*] so early; he was right in recognizing it as a source of the greatest importance since it emanated from the reminiscences of Brother Leo and his companions, and those who had known the saint most intimately."[8] We will return again and again to these texts throughout this book.

Meanwhile, much of what we know of Clare, outside of Thomas of Celano's biography, we have from oral traditions handed down since the friars left her deathbed to continue their work. Some of these stories and legends were recently compiled by the Italian historian Piero Bargellini into his compassionate work *The Little Flowers of Saint Clare*. Bargellini was first and foremost a great Florentine, serving as Councillor for Arts and Gardens, and was in the 1960s the mayor of Florence. But long before that, he was an artist and a writer who wrote influential books on St. Bernadino of Siena, various other aspects of Franciscan spirituality, and Dante.

Along the way to discovering what happened in those early years of the movement, we also will have assistance from various other experts and biographers, including the great nineteenth-century enthusiast for Francis and Clare, Frederick Ozanam. Ozanam (d. 1853) was beatified in 1997 by Pope John Paul II at the Cathedral of Notre Dame in Paris. But long before that day, Ozanam wrote a beautiful book called *The Franciscan Poets of the Thirteenth Century*, first published in English translation in 1914.

Portions of that work are interspersed throughout the chapters below.[9] Ozanam showed how Francis and Clare breathed new life into the spirit of thirteenth-century Italy, and by extension of their followers, the rest of Europe. G. K. Chesterton once said, "St. Francis was very vivid in his poems and rather vague in his documents." Ozanam explains the background and substance of that vividness.

More books have been written about Francis of Assisi than about any other figure in history except Jesus himself. But rarely in those books do readers have an opportunity to assess what Francis actually did that was so extraordinary. The present work will help you to do that. Walk with me through those early years of the movement begun by Brother Francis. See how Sister Clare became his partner, the rudder to his sail, yin to his yang, the other half of the foundation to a spiritual renaissance that transformed Western faith, society, and religion in ways that were threatened, even lost, within their own lifetimes. Explore with me the sometimes simple, sometimes larger, ways that we can live in that original Franciscan spirit today.

We need Francis and Clare today, as much as we ever have. "Our generation already is overpast / Yet love of Christ will win man's love at last." Robert Bridges wrote that simple couplet in memory of his friend Gerard Manley Hopkins nearly a century ago. He was writing about the mistakes of their generation, one that knew the First World War and its accompanying misery and pessimism that was unlike anything their parents had faced. Francis and Clare also lived in a time that felt lost in its myriad conflicts among countries, religions, and classes. Our own day, dawning a new century and millennium, feels similarly overpast.

The Resurrection

We need Francis and Clare today. Our souls and bodies need their wisdom and their sensuous approach to life and spirituality, and we need them to remind us of what it means to take steps toward living like Jesus.

Through our desire to see and touch the risen Christ once again, we are privileged to encounter certain individuals among us who are farther along in their paths toward wholeness, in whom we see much, much more clearly the image of God in Christ. . . . So our penchant for telling stories of those people in whom Christ was born, lived, and died again, this perennial hagiographic impulse of Christianity, so to speak, is inevitably part and parcel of our faith in a risen, incarnate God.[10]

The spirit of the earliest Franciscans is contagious; may we all become infected!

2

ABOUT THEIR
RELATIONSHIP

There are more famous couples from the Middle Ages, but none who had a more profound effect on their time and place than Francis and Clare of Assisi.

In the century before our saints were born, all of Europe knew who Abelard and Heloise were. Heloise was Abelard's student, and Abelard was the most famous theologian of his day. He also liked to claim that he was the only undefeated philosopher in the world. He never lost a debate, and his charisma was undeniable. Abelard and Heloise became lovers, creating a scandal throughout Paris. Heloise gave birth secretly to a son, but soon, the two lovers were forcibly separated by her family. Abelard was violently castrated and exiled, while Heloise entered a convent. But the love letters they exchanged rank among the most poignant in all of literature. Together, they confused the spiritual and secular, a mix of genuine love and serious lust, and the sort of secrecy that marks challenges to power for the wrong reasons.

There are also legends of an earlier famous couple, Benedict of Nursia, the father of Western monasticism and author of his influential *Rule*, and his sister Scholastica. According to Pope

Gregory the Great's famous biography of Benedict, Scholastica represented the female version of all that Benedict strove to be. The most popular story told about the pair is one that seems to recur in the first biographies of Francis and Clare: it is the story of a meal they shared.

According to the legend, Benedict and Scholastica, monk and nun, visited with each other only once a year—and even then they were not alone. Benedict's disciples would accompany them. They would share a meal in a picnic area not far from the monastery gate. But as happens in the stories of saints, Gregory the Great's text explains that spiritual matters took precedent over bodily needs: "They spent the whole day praising God in holy conversation. Night was already falling when they finally took their meal together."[11] This is a recurring theme in the lives of holy men and women: food becomes an afterthought. And, of course, Jesus himself taught that spiritual teachings are more important than daily bread. Gregory continues:

> The evening grew later and later as they sat at the table in holy conversation. Scholastica then made a request: "I beg you, Benedict, not to leave me tonight so that we may talk until morning about the joys of heavenly life." Benedict responded, "What are you talking about? Under no circumstances can I stay outside my cell."

> The heavens were calm and not a single cloud appeared in the sky. When this holy woman heard her brother's refusal, she folded her hands and rested them on the table. She leaned down, put her head on her hands, and prayed to God. When she raised her head, such powerful lightning erupted, and thunder and a flood of rain, that the venerable

Benedict and the brothers with him could not set foot outside the door of where they were sitting. The holy woman had poured out a flood of tears, drawing rain to skies that had been calm.

When Benedict saw that he could not get back to the monastery because of the storm, he was irritated and complained, "God have mercy. Sister, why have you done this?" And she replied to the holy man: "I asked you, and you would not listen. So I asked my Lord, and he has listened."[12]

And so they discussed heaven for the rest of the evening. Scholastica died just three days later.

The medieval imagination was full of these stories by the time that Francis and Clare came along. But unlike Abelard and Heloise, Francis and Clare did not have a physical or sexual relationship. And unlike Benedict and Scholastica, they were not brother and sister. The friendship of Francis and Clare falls somewhere in between. Their story is, in fact, quite complicated.

He was twelve years her elder, and she would have known very little of him before his conversion. As an adolescent, Clare observed Francis's unusual behavior, as he publicly rebelled against his father and the expectations that were placed upon him at home. Then, as a teenager, Clare began to admire him. She heard him preach, and watched as he began his public ministry. She, too, began to doubt the future her family was planning, and she felt the proddings of the Spirit within her. In the bold tradition of women saints who spurned the domestic life,[13] Clare took the radical step of deciding to join Francis and his merry band of men who were transforming the Umbrian hill-towns with their singing and dancing, marriage to *poverty*, and an alternative spiritual path to cloister and hearth. She fled her home one night and joined the Franciscans down in the valley at their modest compound of huts circling the ancient chapel of St. Mary of the Angels.

Francis and Clare then became an unusual couple. The sources all indicate that they had a natural affection for one another. They were not married and they never had an affair, but their love for each other was felt palpably by those around them. G. K. Chesterton calls it a "pure and spiritual romance," an apt description, although they spent very little time together. Clare was an important confidant to Francis, and a link between his childhood, with all of its extravagant worldliness, and the mature, life-changing decisions that began to mark his early twenties. Their affection for and trust of each other fueled the early Franciscan movement and gave birth to a joy, beauty, and spirit that had long been absent from faith.

However, it has always seemed to make for a better story to have Francis and Clare *in love* with each other. Some of the early sources give hints that support such a view. Thomas of Celano, the first biographer of each of them, called theirs a "divine attraction"— these two saints wanting to be together. And when Thomas describes Clare's childhood reputation as a spiritual giant, he also implies that Francis was intent on meeting her. Thomas compares Clare's holiness to plunder, and Francis to a conquering knight. He writes that Francis "was dedicated to snatching his plunder away from the world."

In the canonization proceedings for Clare that happened just after her death, one of Clare's sisters testified that it was Francis who made the first visit to see Clare, while she was still a teenager living in her father's house. Given Francis's apostolic life at that time, and the way in which marriages were usually prearranged by parents, this seems highly unlikely. The events were more than forty years in the past when Clare's sister was remembering them. Could it be that she remembered things in this way because the values of the day stated that a woman could not make such contact with a man outside her family? There may have been some intent to preserve the family reputation.

According to *The Acts of the Process of Canonization of St. Clare*, written by Thomas of Celano in 1253, Francis and Clare did indeed meet several times before her conversion, and on one occasion the text reads that Clare snuck away clandestinely to hear him preach. But there is no hint of dating or flirting in these passages. Francis was twelve years older than Clare. When he was going through his first dramatic moments of conversion she was barely twelve. She was fourteen when Francis renounced his father and all his wealth in the public square before the bishop and all of Assisi. And when Clare later came to join Francis's movement in the dead of night, her heart and stomach would have been full of terror—not the excitement one feels before a first kiss! They were friends, and they shared a kinship that was more important than romance.

Fifty years ago, Nikos Kazantzakis, the Greek novelist, made popular the notion that Francis and Clare shared a relationship that was sexually charged. In *Saint Francis*,[14] Kazantzakis had the book's narrator, Brother Leo, say to his spiritual father:

> I am the only one . . . who knows about your carnal love for Count Favorini Scifi's daughter Clara. All the others, because they are afraid of their own shadows, think you loved only her soul. But it was her body that you loved

earliest of all; it was from there that you set out, got your start. Then, after struggle, struggle against the devil's snares, you were able with God's help to reach her soul. You loved that soul, but without ever denying her body, and without ever touching it either.[15]

According to Kazantzakis, Clare was one of the girls whom Francis had wooed like a troubadour before his conversion, singing at her windows from the street below. When Clare later came to the Portiuncula in the middle of the night in order to become the first woman Franciscan, she urged Francis to believe that she wanted to love only God. "Last night I heard you calling me by name. It was you, Father Francis. You were standing beneath my window once more and calling me. 'Come! Come! Come!' you said. So, I came."[16] Francis then tried to flee. He was scared of his own latent lust, despite the fact that, by this time in the novel, Francis had almost completely lost his eyesight. But the other friars compelled Francis to stay and listen to the pleading of Clare. And so he did, and he began to interrogate her. Can you really go about town barefoot? Can you, a woman from a wealthy home, stomach feeling hungry? Will you, the daughter of a count, be willing to beg for your bread? And Clare answered affirmatively to every question. "I can, I can," she said, but Francis retorted, "You cannot!"

Kazantzakis had Francis participating in the ancient subjugation of women, believing women to be less than men in intellect, spirit, and honesty. He had Francis say, "I don't trust you women. Eve's serpent has been licking your ears and lips for too many centuries. Do not lead me into temptation. Other ladies will gather around you, and you'll all climb up to the convent roof to ogle the brothers. . . . No, get up and return home. We don't want women!"[17]

What a shame! We could psychoanalyze this novelist and come up with explanations for why he made his saints so confused (remember the schizophrenic Jesus of *The Last Temptation of Christ*?), but suffice it to say that it probably did not happen that way.[18] It is true that saints often disappoint us, but it is also true that we disappoint the saints, particularly when we assume sexual relationships for them where there were none. Why do we seem to want our holy men and women to have sexual experiences? Perhaps sex becomes the simplest path to understanding them as like ourselves. Nowhere is this more evident than in the current, but also medieval, fascination surrounding Jesus and Mary Magdalene. More than a millennium and a half before Dan Brown ever conceived *The Da Vinci Code*, Origen's theological opponent, Celsus, suggested that the Magdalene and Christ were lovers. There are even debates as to whether or not Martin Luther may have said something similar. A decade ago, a liberal American Episcopal bishop, John Shelby Spong, wrote that Mary Magdalene may have been married to Jesus and subsequently bore his children. But just as there is only a fraction of evidence to suggest such things—compared to the evidence to support the more conventional views—so, too, there is little reason to believe that Francis and Clare shared any romance other than one that was jointly with God.

After Kazantzakis, Italian director Franco Zeffirelli created his film *Brother Sun, Sister Moon* (1972), in which Francis and Clare are portrayed as young romantics who turn an interest in each other into a mutual interest in the spiritual life. In the first scene of the film, featuring Alec Guinness as Pope Innocent III, the twenty-year-old Francis playfully chases the young teenager Clare as she makes her way to a lonely grotto bringing food to some outcast lepers. Francis is horrified when he sees the lepers and he runs off. The next time they are together on screen, they gaze at each other as Francis marches off to war. Their third scene is in a field of poppies on a sunny afternoon; they have a sweet conversation as Francis's parents eavesdrop and discuss a possible marriage. Later in the film, when Clare comes in the middle of the night to join Francis's movement, *Brother Sun, Sister Moon* shows a scene almost bubbling over with erotic energy that is being turned to spiritual ends.[19]

The myths of Kazantzakis and Zeffirelli have warped the imagination of a generation of those who would be interested in learning about Francis and Clare. How are historians to compete with a best-selling novel and a hit movie? There is something compelling about unrequited love, especially erotic love that seems somehow forbidden. Some modern biographers have even led readers down this path, driven either by the desire to tell a compelling story, or simply to connect the story with the prevalent myth. Gloria Hutchinson writes that the beginning of the Poor Clares was the same as that "romantic scene idealized by Franco Zeffirelli in *Brother Sun, Sister Moon*."[20] One of the best recent biographies of Francis declares, "Clare may have fallen in love with Francis at first, as many believe she did."[21] And another of the most important communicators of the spirituality of Francis and Clare has suggested that it was romantic love that drew them together:

> She had known almost at once that she would follow him.
> . . . She soon learned, however, that they could never be

together, for then they would not be free, they would not
be who they really were, two pilgrims in love with the
Lord, two souls who were closer apart than they could ever
be together. Together they might end up loving each other
more than the treasure they had found in one another's
heart.[22]

They were two strong, magnetic personalities who could
communicate with each other easily by glance, note, or shared
prayer, whether they were in the same place at the same time or
not. They were likely together on fewer than a dozen occasions
over the space of twenty years, most of them only for a matter
of hours. But they understood each other, supported each other,
and complemented each other's strengths and weaknesses.

The great Spanish mystic and philosopher Miguel de
Unamuno once wrote: "Even in the purest realm of the spirit,
without the shadow of any vice, man seeks support in woman,
as Francis of Assisi did in Clare."[23] This is very similar to Genesis
2, when God says, "It is not good that the man should be alone;
I will make him a helper as his partner." They were friends who
felt a kinship in passion for turning away from the world and
following Christ. They shared a feeling that their parents could
not understand how they felt about the future and what it meant
to be successful. There were likely no romantic yearnings and
surely no sexual relationship between Francis and Clare. They
did not have a relationship *past* that need interest us. When
Francis cut Clare's hair (as a sign of her tonsure, or promise to
live for Christ) on that fascinating first evening—after she had
run away from home to join him and the friars—there was no
scent of perfume in the air. Clare was immediately a *brother*.

TO KISS A LEPER

I f history teaches us anything, it is how similar human weaknesses have been throughout the ages. Human foibles, faults, and wickedness wind a pattern throughout the history of civilization. Human beings are as similar to one another in weakness as are great religious figures in strength and wisdom. Across the religious traditions, we see how the exemplars of all faiths have had to overcome basic tendencies toward greed, self-preservation, lust, laziness, and many another sins recounted in stories and scriptures. Saints are taught, not born.

The best teacher of Francis Bernardone was the Holy Spirit at work in his own conscience. In the beginning, in his early twenties, Francis began to spend time alone for the first time. He drew away from the childhood friends who had previously engaged his lusts for fame and friendship, and he wandered to deserted places in the Umbrian hillsides. Francis was particularly drawn to abandoned churches—and there were many of them in thirteenth-century Italy. We can see in him the medieval feeling of devotion simply upon entering a church. These quiet spaces made possible other divine action within him.

If Francis had not finally felt the need to be by himself after years of teenage waste and solipsism, what happened in him next would have been impossible. On the path to conversion it is necessary to have the space, quiet, and freedom to see ourselves more clearly for what we really are. Francis began to see who he was and then, with God's help, to see what was possible in a human being, instead. This is one of the common features of all saints: they have private relationships with God. Their closet expressions—quiet, uncomplicated, and alone with God—become the foundation for the sanctity that they later show.

Francis began to give of himself to others. Thomas of Celano[24] tells us that he followed the example of St. Martin of Tours and gave his clothes to a destitute knight who had lost his own garments and armor in a recent battle. But, where St. Martin had cut his cloak in two, giving half of it to a beggar, Francis radicalized the commitment of a follower of Jesus and stripped completely, removing those "fine, tailored clothes" of his father's for one of the last times. Jesus said: "[I]f someone wishes to go to law with you to get your tunic, let him have your cloak as well. And if anyone requires you to go one mile, go two miles with him."[25] This sort of self-sacrifice became a pattern with Francis, and the occasions for it usually began in simple times of solitude.

Other steps followed on the path toward Francis's becoming, again in the words of Thomas, "a different person." The changes within him were the same sort of qualitative difference that happened in the New Testament story of Saul becoming Paul, or that can be seen in any saint since the biblical era who has been transformed from world-centered to Christ-centered. Francis's decisions were being transformed by a desire to do the right thing, or God's will, which he determined by reading the Gospels. He became self-critical and was able to see his former, unconverted life as dissipate. He found various means of repentance and penance. Saints help others toward conversion with their easy understanding of sin, as well as their awareness of what it means to be released from sin.

Francis's conversion next found expression in his recognizing the inequality that existed between the advantaged and the disadvantaged, the healthy and the ailing, and the loved and the loveless. The love of God began to build in his heart, and God's love gradually replaced the loves that Francis had previously held with ardor for things of the world. To his rollicking friends he soon seemed distant and less enjoyable to be around. As he became more solitary, he began to exhibit moments of divine inspiration. The notion of what might happen in future events, and an awareness of human motives, all became more accessible. This is another aspect of sanctity that appears miraculous to those of us on the outside looking in, but is, in reality, more common than we think. Saints have developed heightened sensitivities to and perceptions of the thoughts, desires, and needs of those around them. This ability may be more common than is typically imagined.

At about this time, he walked to Rome—no small feat for a man in Umbria. But a pilgrimage during the Middle Ages was meant to be slowly traveled, usually on foot, or perhaps riding a horse or a donkey. All indications are that Francis walked with a few companions, but in spirit he was very alone with God during those early days.

While in Rome, they visited the Church of St. Peter. These were the days before the great basilica that was built during the Renaissance, adorned with the work of Michelangelo. The site was the anciently meaningful one where St. Peter had been martyred in Nero's Circus some thirty years after Christ's crucifixion. A small church—a shrine, really, erected in the third century—was called

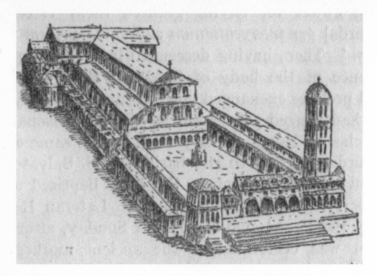

The medieval St. Peter's Basilica in Rome

Prince of the Apostles. But by the fourth century, the first St. Peter's Basilica was built by the Emperor Constantine. It was there that Charlemagne was crowned Holy Roman Emperor on Christmas Day, AD 800, by Pope Leo III. Lothair, Louis II, and Frederick III were similarly crowned by popes in that space. It was this St. Peter's—not the renovated and expanded one that caused Martin Luther to begin his attack on Pope Leo X in the early 1500s—that Francis was visiting. Again, Francis stripped off his fine clothes, but this time, he exchanged his garments with the sundry ones of a beggar who sat in front of the great church.

Francis still possessed a great deal of money at this time. We know this because he gladly made a large offering of coins while visiting the usual pilgrimage sites in Rome. He had always been the boy who was fun to have around because of the money in his pockets, but on this occasion, the money began to spill in the direction of the needy.

All of these conversion experiences culminated one day when Francis, back in Assisi, approached a leper while riding his horse. The leper of the thirteenth century was a vagrant, cast out from society as well as from church. Leprosy was incurable at this time, and those who were afflicted were anathema. Lepers were the same incurable, contagious outcasts as they had been in Jesus' time. First-century Palestine and thirteenth-century Italy were both pre-science. The common response to the disease was inherited from ancient days going back to Leviticus 13:45–46: "The person who has the leprous disease shall wear torn clothes and let the hair of his head be disheveled; and he shall cover his upper lip and cry out, 'Unclean, unclean.' He shall remain unclean as long as he has the disease; he is unclean. He shall live alone; his dwellings shall be outside the camp."

During the Middle Ages, local priests performed a ceremony in which the priest would recite: "I forbid you to enter church, monastery, fair, mill, marketplace or tavern. . . . I forbid you ever to leave your house without your leper's costume . . . to live with any woman other than your own . . . to touch a well, or well cord, without your gloves . . . to touch children, or to give them anything . . . to eat or drink, except with lepers."[26] Lazarus was the patron saint of lepers in the Middle Ages because, although the Gospels do not diagnose him as a leper, the symptoms appear to be unmistakable when he is described in Luke's Gospel: "There was a rich man who used to dress in purple and fine linen. . . . And at his gate there used to lie a poor man called Lazarus, covered with sores, who longed to fill himself with what fell from the rich man's table. Even dogs came and licked his sores."[27]

Leprosy is actually still with us, although not in Palestine or Umbria. Somewhere between one and three million cases of leprosy are to be found in Brazil, India, Madagascar, Mozambique, Myanmar (formerly Burma), and Nepal. We know today that the disease is treatable and only mildly contagious. The kind of physical contact that the first Franciscans boldly had with lepers will rarely if ever result in transferring the disease. But Francis did not know that.

Francis knew that Jesus had cared for lepers. Ten lepers, according to Luke's Gospel, "approached him. Keeping their distance, they called out, saying, 'Jesus, Master, have mercy on us!'" In healing them, Jesus showed his willingness to look at, speak to, and befriend those that the rest of humankind had deemed unclean and sinful.

Lepers became the final test of Francis's conversion. We are told that there was nothing that frightened young Bernardone more than a leper. When he approached the leper while riding his horse near Assisi, his first instinct was to avoid him; he rode past the man feeling a sickening revulsion in his stomach. But then he brought his beast to an abrupt stop. He dismounted and ran back to the leper, grabbed the man by the shoulders—and kissed him! Legend tells us that Francis then remounted his horse only to turn back and see that the man had disappeared!

Was the leper a divine messenger, sent to test Francis? Was he only the object of a dream? Francis worried for many days that he had only been dreaming. Perhaps the test was not real and perhaps then Francis's "passing the test," so to speak, was also then not real. Sometimes when you want something so desperately your imagination runs faster than your life's actions themselves. With all of his heart, Francis wanted to be holy, to purge himself of sinfulness and to replace it with goodness.

The *Second Life* of Thomas of Celano tells us that Francis then set out to find more lepers. He rode and walked to their caves and huts, tucked away in places not intended for visiting, and gave them coins and kisses. Sometimes he would take along a companion, we are told in *The Legend of the Three Companions*, another early text, and after caring for the lepers Francis would leave his companion to go inside a cave and pray alone. "Inspired by a new, special spirit, he prayed to his Father in secret, wanting to keep secret what he knew was happening inside of him."[28] It was the contact with lepers that culminated in his conversion, according to Thomas of Celano: *mutatus perfecte iam corde* in the original Latin, or "a perfect change of heart."

Francis's care for lepers may remind us also of what Jesus did after his death and before his resurrection. The Apostle's Creed says simply, "He descended into hell." Some theologians (such as the reformer John Calvin) have explained that Christ's descent into hell was largely metaphoric, symbolizing the spiritual and physical torment that he underwent on our behalf. But more compelling is the interpretation that Christ actually descended into a physical place called Hell in order to demonstrate that releasing people from sin includes releasing them from pain. Psalm 107 foreshadows this sort of Messiah: "He brought them out of darkness and gloom / and broke their bonds asunder. / Let them thank the LORD for his steadfast love, / for his wonderful works to humankind. / For he shatters the doors of bronze / and cuts in two the bars of iron."

POVERTY BOTH ROMANTIC AND LITERAL

Above all else, Francis wanted to be poor. Embracing those with leprosy was his first step into a multifaceted *marriage* to poverty.

Francis and Clare combined romance and idealism in their lives together with a stark literalism. The most obvious example of Francis's romantic side is seen just after his conversion, when he wed himself to what he called "Lady Poverty." As Clare would later do, Francis said that he took a different spouse than was expected of him. Expressed throughout his writings, his love for Lady Poverty shows the heart of a romantic and the spirit of a troubadour. Umberto Eco describes this spirit: "The formation of symbols was artistic. To decipher them was to experience them aesthetically. It was a type of aesthetic expression in which the Medievals took great pleasure in deciphering puzzles, in spotting the daring analogy, in feeling that they were involved in adventure and discovery."[29] Lady Poverty was Francis's primary symbol, puzzle, analogy, and adventure. His love for the feelings of human love was transformed into a love for the love of God.

Francis was not actually the first troubadour-turned-religious. Folquet of Marseille composed many troubadour songs in the 1180s and 1190s, only to quit his amorous ways and become a Cistercian monk, and later a bishop. There were also stories in the reverse. Most of the love poets known as the Goliards were, in fact, professed religious in rebellion. They wrote verses ridiculing the institutions of the Church and mocking the sometimes poor relationship between piety and reality in the lives of the religious.

The Marriage of St. Francis and Poverty

But just as Francis enjoyed the drama of being *married* to Lady Poverty, he was also literal in his pursuit of *voluntary* poverty—both as a personal commitment and as a community guideline for his brothers and Clare and the sisters. He resisted every effort of his brothers to own even the most reasonable things: spiritual books, worship manuals, buildings for sleeping, churches. His vision was to be completely like Christ, who told the first disciples to go about preaching without anything for the journey. All would be provided, Christ said, including daily food and future clothing. Francis severely punished friars who even touched coins; they became unclean in his model for faith just as lepers became washed in God's love; and he forbade anyone from preparing food that was intended to be eaten tomorrow.

As all true knights were devoted to the service of some lady, Francis had to choose his. Indeed, a few days before his conversion, when his friends found him wrapped in thought and asked him if he were thinking of taking a wife, Francis replied: "It is true I am contemplating taking the noblest, richest, and most beautiful lady that ever lived." This was the description he gave of his ideal, the type of all moral beauty, Lady Poverty.

He loved to personify this virtue according to the symbolic genius of his time. He imagined her as a heavenly damsel, then the lady of his thoughts, his betrothed, his spouse. He gave to her all the power which the troubadours attributed to the noble ladies celebrated in their poems—the power of wresting from the souls captivated by her all worldly thoughts and inclinations, of elevating such souls to the society of angels. But to the troubadours these platonic loves were merely witticisms, while the invisible beauty that had ravished St. Francis wrung from him the most impassioned

Francis enjoyed the expressions of faith that would cause others to take notice, but he also desired to make himself despised, an anti-hero, on many occasions. He once insisted that his good friend Brother Bernard step on his face, as punishment. He later singed his flesh when tempted toward lust, and rolled naked in the snow to get rid of temptation. He smiled while being ridiculed by the young boys of Assisi in the early days of his conversion. There is very little that is sweet about this side of Francis. He could be as literally minded as some of the more radical reformers who came after him.

His commitment to being reviled reminds me of the teachings of the Danish philosopher Søren Kierkegaard. What are the qualities of those whom God chooses for a special life, such as that of a saint? The answer is more ordinary than we might think: We don't earn God's favor, and we are not predisposed toward sanctity. Kierkegaard explains that if you are considered righteous by others, if you are regularly invited to be in a position of leadership in your church, if everyone admires and respects you—it isn't Jesus Christ that you are tracking. In contrast to centuries of teaching as to what the "personality" of sainthood might be, Kierkegaard says instead: "It appears that to be a Christian, to belong truly to Christ . . . in truth should mean in the world, in the eyes of men, to be abased, that it should mean all possible hardships, every possible sort of derision and insult, and mean at last to be punished as a criminal!"[30]

cries. Open any of the medieval poets and you will find no song more bold, no words more impassioned, than this prayer of the penitent of Assisi: "O my most sweet Lord Jesus Christ, have pity on me and on my Lady Poverty, for I burn with love for her, and without her I cannot rest. O my Lord, who did cause me to love her, you know that she is sitting in sadness, rejected by all."

—*Frederick Ozanam*

Francis felt emotions deeply, and identified with people intimately, in ways that resulted in the sort of active love that is called *charity* in the epistles of St. Paul. Like one of the Japanese priests in Shusaku Endo's famous novel *Silence*, Francis knew the difference between empathy and this deeper sort of love: "His pity for them had been overwhelming; but pity was not action. It was not love. Pity, like passion, was no more than a kind of instinct."[31] Early Franciscan poverty was the ground that caused charity to grow. Francis understood how money and ownership breed competition and jealousy, and how owning nothing makes it possible to give unreservedly because one has nothing to lose.

These were the practical bases for early Franciscan poverty. A friar who owns land feels obliged to use it properly by building a suitable house. A house will include the tools of worship, statuary, crafted windows, candlesticks, books, and resources for instructing others in the faith. These things need defending from possible intruders. And so, even a modest religious house becomes one with a degree of wealth that makes men prepared to hurt those who would attempt to take it from them.

Francis and Clare did not believe, as did some heretics during the Middle Ages, that the world was essentially bad, or evil, or alien. Heretical groups such as the Cathars preached that poverty was essential in order to separate oneself from the earth and the things of creation. A Cathar would no more own land than he would enjoy a good meal or admire a flower. Francis and Clare were optimists and idealists in combination with their literalism, and they found joy in voluntary poverty. Their voluntary poverty had everything to do with freedom and nothing to do with separation. As one eloquent Franciscan puts it today, "While the world is filled with God's overflowing goodness, it is poverty that allows one to experience this goodness by becoming radically dependent on God."[32]

Poverty was also, quite simply, the way to be like Jesus. God's becoming a human being was an act of profound, voluntary poverty. But then, on the level of detail, both Francis and Clare believed that it was not an accident of history that there was no room in the inn. The swaddling clothes and manger (an animal's feeding trough) were no accident either, for this different sort of king. The public ministry of Jesus was unsuccessful by worldly standards; he had twelve men and two or three women with him before his passion; at the Cross, he had only his mother and John. None of these facts were accidents. They were all evidences of the voluntary poverty of Jesus. Every fact about the life of Christ was intended to teach an aspect of Francis and Clare's new way of life.

With Francis and Clare, the Christian became mendicant, homeless, and homely. That's what being married to poverty was all about. In all these things they imitated Christ. Francis became the poor Christ in the actions of his life, while Clare—due to the accident of thirteenth-century European history that said women could not live apostolic lives beside men—became the poor Christ in contemplation. So, as Francis teaches us what to *do*, Clare shows us how to *be*. Both of them made Jesus visible, audible, and recognizable through their lives.

CHAPTER 4

REBUILDING THE CHURCH

S till wearing his father's fine clothing but questioning almost everything, Francis Bernardone left Assisi by the city gate known as Porta Nuova and wandered aimlessly into the hot sun that bathes the hillside as it winds down away from town. Fresh from his experience of kissing the leper, Francis was full of excitement. Thomas of Celano claims with a hagiographer's bravado that "his heart was already completely changed."[33] That is doubtful. Francis still had thoughts of his former friends, who were nipping at his heels most days and nights in hopes of returning him to a life of frivolity. Most of them would soon fade into the distance completely, and none would ever join Francis in his new life.

Bonaventure says that the sensitive young man "sought lonely places, dear only to mourners," which is to put too dour a spin on it. The romantic sought out rocky paths, dilapidated buildings, ancient castles, and ruins, all of which stoked his imagination in ways that books or conversation may enflame the thoughts of others less sensuous.

He visited the fallen church of San Damiano again and again during those early days, probably both before his brief sojourn as a knight gone off to war against Perugia, and then afterwards, when he had come back home in disgrace. He walked there on many days when his father did not require his help in the shop. He walked there on many days when his mother believed, or perhaps hoped, that he was instead off to see some girl. He did not yet have an idea of what his vocation was to be.

San Damiano was probably tended by a priest, but a poor or absent-minded one. It was a church without much of a congregation and without the sort of appointments that made other churches in Assisi great. The building was in the beginning stages of ruin, but that is exactly why Francis felt drawn to it. Certain places imprint themselves on us and make us feel completely present in something larger, as if our lives are a jigsaw puzzle and the discovered place holds one of our missing pieces.

It is intriguing that we don't have accounts of Francis talking with the priest of San Damiano, asking for advice regarding his life's direction. Instead, it is the altar that drew him, and the icon that hung above it. That icon of Christ on the cross was one of the most striking in all of Umbria. Francis looked into the eyes of Christ there, feeling absolutely sure that they were the eyes of God, looking back at him. He looked at icons as medieval people did; he was wandering down to San Damiano so often because he wanted to *be seen* by Christ.

Even Martin Luther, a medieval man in many ways, later understood what it meant to look deeply at, and be transformed by, an image of Christ: "Through mercy and grace, Christ on the cross removes thy sins from thee, carries them, and strangles them; keep this always in mind and doubt it not—this means, look at this holy image and make it thy own."[34] It was in these moments—which turned into hours—that Francis began to yearn to be like the One who was looking back at him. Francis knew very little of the life of Jesus at this point in his life, but he began to learn the stories and the teachings, perhaps sometimes from the lonely priest of San Damiano.

On one special occasion, Francis was alone in the chapel: Bonaventure says that he was lying prostrate on the floor; other texts written by Francis's closest friends simply record that Francis had gone into the church to pray. No one was with Francis to observe what happened next. Bonaventure wrote that what happened caused Francis to lose consciousness for a time, in a mystical ecstasy; but again, other texts make it sound less miraculous, more important. He heard a voice speak to him from the icon (which now hangs in the side chapel of the Basilica of St. Clare of Assisi) and believed it to be the voice of Christ.

When Francis returned from the abandoned church, having just heard the voice of God, he had no one to whom he could tell his story. He was almost completely alone. Bonaventure says, "The servant of the Most High had no one to instruct him except Christ." Later, he would tell his first companions that Christ simply said to him: "Francis, go and repair my house, which, as you can see, is falling down."

The Legend of the Three Companions—written by friars Angelo, Leo, and Rufinus almost twenty years before Bonaventure's official *Life*—tells us that it was this moment before the cross of San Damiano that initiated Francis's identification with Christ and, in particular, with his passion. Could it be that Francis was seeking a connection to the institutional Church when he prayed before icons in churches? Perhaps he wanted God to tell him what to do, how to be a Christian of true commitment, and he expected a different answer. Francis sought a *connection*, to be sure, but was it spiritual only, or ecclesiastical as well? When he received his word from God, he did not run off and join a monastic order. That's an important piece of information.

Joining the Benedictines or the Cistercians would have been the most logical thing for a young man to do in circumstances like Francis's, fresh from a private communication from God. But Francis knew, as did everyone at the time, of the massive corruption in the Church. He began his work, instead, in a mendicant, reform tradition (epitomized by Peter Waldo and Joachim of Fiore a few decades earlier), only tangentially related at first to the Catholic Church. Francis left San Damiano with his mission in mind, and he plunged his hands in both pockets and gave every coin to the attendant priest, who happened to be nearby. He was on his first mission: to literally repair the fallen chapel.

The Thirteenth-century Church

The century before Francis was born was one of the most corrupt in the history of the Christian Church. The pursuit of or hold on power and influence, as well as the desire for economic gain or security, were often the factors that led to decisions being made. Power brokering was more important than spiritual matters or doctrinal teaching. It was so bad in those days that it was often said that the majority of parish priests and bishops were practicing either simony (extorting money), keeping prostitutes, or both. They were not just corruptible and prone to adultery, but they were extortionists and worse.

One of the reasons for which the first Franciscans were important to their era is that their reforms of poverty and simplicity were so necessary for reforming the Church. One trustworthy early friar, Salimbene of Parma, explained in very frank language:

> I have found some priests lending out their money to usury and enriching themselves merely for the sake of their bastards: again, I have found others keeping taverns . . . and spending their nights in sin, and celebrating Mass next day. And when the people communicate, [the priests] thrust the consecrated hosts which remain over into clefts of the wall: though these are the very body of our Lord. And many other foul things they do and horrible to be told, which I pass over for brevity's sake.[35]

Salimbene's life bridged the time between the end of Francis's life (he was born five years before the saint's death) and the quarter century of Clare's life that followed. Salimbene came to know many of the first religious friends of Francis, including Bernard of Quintavalle, the first disciple. Salimbene writes often of Bernard, "with whom I dwelt for a whole winter in the Convent of Siena. He was my familiar friend. To me and other young men he would recount many marvels concerning the blessed Francis. Much good have I heard and learned from him."[36] His recording of the Church's corruption was damning. Salimbene offers many colorful, descriptive portraits of those who were using the Church for personal ends. Most memorable is the corruption of one of the bishops of Parma, a self-professed nonbeliever who even refused deathbed rites, saying that he had been bishop only for the money.[37] Abbot Guibert of Nogent wrote in France at about the same time: "What can I say? Not even monks, let alone the secular clergy, abstain from raising funds under suspicious circumstances, or shrink from speaking heresies on matters of faith in my presence in order to do the same."

The situation in France and Italy was such that it could not even be covered up. There was widespread opinion among the good elements of Church leadership that the pope must deal severely with the rotten characters, but there was also fear that sanctions would be so widespread as to induce the faithful into the heresy known as Donatism, a rejection of the Church because of the bad elements in it. This was the late Middle Ages: the Church stood at the center of public life; religion—which in these communities was only Christianity—was not a private affair, but a series of public pieties and obligations, all of which ran through local priests and bishops for their authority. Nevertheless, in encyclicals published between 1074 and 1109, Pope Gregory VII told all Christians that they must reject the sacraments given from the hands of corrupt priests. These letters, sent out into the parishes and read aloud in public squares, caused riots.

Six different popes ruled this troubled Church, spread across two continents, from the time of Francis's birth to the time of his conversion twenty-four years later. These were difficult times, which led to consolidations of power. During Francis's and Clare's lifetimes, the bishop of Rome became more and more influential in the lives of Western Christians. At almost precisely the time that Francis began his conversion, the bishop of Rome took on the spiritual power and responsibility that

*The Pope's Dream (when Innocent III dreamed
that Francis would hold up a falling church)*

has marked popes ever since. He became the sole person who officially denotes sainthood, speaks with final doctrinal authority, and blesses new movements. Innocent III (1198–1216), the pope who first gave permission to Francis's movement, is the one who claimed these real powers for all future popes by saying: "We are the successor of the prince of the Apostles [Peter], but we are not his vicar, not the vicar of any man or Apostle, but the vicar of Jesus Christ himself."[38]

Despite all of these troubles in the churches, bishops and popes rarely garner mention in texts such as *The Little Flowers* or *The Mirror of Perfection*. Instead, we hear of friars, farmers, lepers, revelers, rambunctious children, merchants, and other common folk. It is clear where Francis's priorities and those of the friars who followed most closely in his footsteps lay. From the earliest days of his conversion, Francis spent relatively little time worrying about what Rome thought of his actions. His relationship to the Church was always one of an obedient son who nevertheless tried to keep himself removed from its centers and people of power. He could see the ways in which papal authority could change the ideals of a religious movement. When Francis's contemporary St. Dominic was frequently heading to Rome for talks with cardinals and popes, Francis was usually avoiding the trip. Rarely do we see Francis running to his local bishop, or to Rome, for permission to do something. His attention lay elsewhere, but also, he knew better than to always be asking.

But soon after the saint's death, his Order entered the arena of religious politics and power struggles, competing with Benedictines, Dominicans, and Cistercians. When a Franciscan entered into a dispute with a university colleague, landowner, or civil authority, or was accused by the Inquisition of doctrinal or moral error, the resolution of the dispute rested largely on who had the more powerful support in Rome. Whom you knew became the test of who was right. This was not true in Francis's day. Francis was wary of any friar's pursuing power or influence of any kind. In fact, he would not have liked that a Franciscan, Nicholas IV, became pope within a generation of his death (1288), or that another, John Peckam, became the archbishop of Canterbury (1279–1292).

When Francis turned to do as Christ told him at San Damiano—"go and repair my house, which, as you can see, is falling down"—he did not have in mind ways of fixing these big problems within the Church. That would have been impossible for him. Instead, he understood himself as one simple man who could easily do as God told him to do: repair churches, one by one, with his hands. He did not begin a funding campaign. He did not begin a recruitment effort, seeking helpers. He began gathering stones, which was difficult work for such a small man. As *The Legend of the Three Companions* relates, "he had been very refined while living in his father's house."[39] Francis began the task of rebuilding churches, starting with San Damiano itself. G. K. Chesterton writes:

> He went about by himself collecting stones. He begged all the people he met to give him stones. In fact he became a new sort of beggar, reversing the parable; a beggar who asks not for bread but a stone. Probably, as happened to him again and again throughout his extraordinary existence, the very queerness of the request gave it a sort of popularity; and all sorts of idle and luxurious people fell in with the benevolent project, as they would have done with a bet.[40]

He, in fact, never left behind the task of maintaining churches. Even in his later years, Francis would always carry a broom when he went off to preach in a church. He would preach and then sweep the floor clean.[41]

CHAPTER
5

WHO IS MY FATHER?

There is a startling tradition in history of young men and women spurning their fathers (and sometimes their mothers) for service to God alone. Francis stole from his father in order to give to the poor, and then, when confronted about his wrongdoing in the public square before the bishop of Assisi, refused to repent. Isn't repenting what a saint would have been expected to do? Apparently not, according to the early texts. Neither Thomas of Celano nor Bonaventure nor any of the early companions question Francis's motives, although it is mentioned that the priest of San Damiano, to whom Francis wanted to give the money, would not accept it.

Francis's actions in the piazza were a surprise to all who witnessed them, and this is why the story comes down to us with such drama and intensity. Francis turned his back completely on his family, stripping naked and leaving even the clothes off his back as payment of his earthly debt to his father. He shocked his contemporaries not only by his extravagant commitment to God, expressed profoundly for the first time in that public confrontation, but through the plain rejection of his father. Francis said before everyone in town: "Until this moment, I have called you my father, but from this point forward I will confidently say, 'Our Father, Who art in heaven.'

It is with God my Father that I have laid up my treasure and with whom I have fastened my entire hope and trust.'"[42] The son disowned the father.

There is no question that all of this would have brought tremendous shame on Peter Bernardone, as well as suspicion on the son. But there are no apologies from the early biographers. Before the encounter between father and son, in fact, *The Legend of the Three Companions* emphasizes that Francis spent time fasting and weeping, both symbols of a saint's asking for God's guidance, "casting his hope completely on the Lord, who in turn, filled him with inexpressible joy and shone before him as a marvelous light."[43]

After the public demonstration against the father, we also never again hear of Francis's mother. In the life of a saint as sensitive as Francis, it seems unusual that we would know almost nothing about his mother. Surely, a converted man would still have room in his life to love his mother, a woman who, it seems, protected him more than once from the wrath of her husband. After his son had stolen those garments from his shop and sold them to give the money to the poor, Peter Bernardone beat him and locked him in the cellar of the family home, according to tradition. Tourists to Assisi can still see the place where Francis's childhood home once stood, and outside it there is a statue depicting his father and mother; his mother appears holding broken chains that symbolize how she freed him while her husband was away. Bonaventure tells it this way: "After a little time, after the father's departing, his mother—who disliked her husband's ways of dealing with their son—freed Francis from his bonds, and let him go from the house." There is no mention then that Francis thanked his mother, embraced her, or even spoke with her. Instead, "Francis gave thanks to the Lord Almighty, and returned to the place where he had been before."[44] Thomas of Celano recorded years later how Francis picked his spiritual brother, Elias, as "the one he chose to be as a mother to himself."[45] The son disowned his mother, as well.

This may be the most dramatic case in history of a son's sinning against his father, completely dismissing both father and mother, and yet going on to become a tremendous saint. And yet, the ambiguities go unmentioned by Francis's early biographers.

Throughout the late Middle Ages, the primary model for a troubled relationship between father and son was the parable of the prodigal son as told in Luke 15. Abundant visual images and narrative retellings of this parable at the time of Francis's conversion demonstrate that the story dominated the imagination of people. The lesson of the parable would have included the idea that penitence and reconciliation were the prescriptions for wayward sons—not the sort of grandstanding that Francis did.

Some of the first Gothic cathedrals featured stained-glass windows that told the parable of the prodigal son. These were erected during the difficult years of Francis's conversion. The parable had become—just at the time of Francis's coming up— one of the most popular iconographic representations of what it means to sin and then find redemption. The benevolent father of the tale told by Jesus was likened to God the Father, who, no matter what a young sinner may do, is ready and waiting and willing to receive. Francis likely never saw the stained-glass windows installed at the Chartres (1200), Sens (1207), Bourges (1210), or Poitiers (1210) cathedrals—featuring tellings of the popular parable—but he was deliberately acting contrary to what had become a popular expression of the relationship between fathers and sons.[46] Why wouldn't the Assisi bishop, the priest of San Damiano, or later, Pope Innocent III, have asked Francis to reconcile with his father? In the parable, the prodigal son, after squandering his inheritance, is reduced to caring for pigs and even to eating what they eat, for he has nothing left. Finally, he decides to travel back home and ask his father's forgiveness.

According to the pedagogy of Jesus' parable, Francis could have squandered away his father's wealth (by selling the stolen cloth) but then returned home to ask forgiveness. If things had gone that way, it would have also meant re-imagining the time that Francis spent in between the selling of the cloth and facing his father before the bishop. Some of the texts say that that period of time was as long as a month, as Francis hid from his father, fasting and weeping and so on, before gaining the confidence to face him. What was seen as wallowing with pigs became something saintly, for Francis. The father of the biblical parable says to his servants after embracing his son who has returned from sin, "Bring the calf we have been fattening, and kill it; we will celebrate by having a feast." Francis did nothing of the kind. Instead, he would have his heavenly Father say this to him, rather than his earthly one. Other teachings of Jesus tell us that the heavenly host rejoices when even one sinner repents (Luke 15:7). It would seem, though, that Francis had no need to repent. But why?

By the time his father confronted him before the bishop, Francis knew his Gospels well enough to know that he was rebelling against his parents in a way that was similar to what Jesus himself had done. In Luke's Gospel we find the scene of Jesus as a twelve-year-old boy in the temple in Jerusalem, when he stayed behind to talk with the scholars and priests against the wishes of his parents. After searching for him for three days in a strange city, Mary found Jesus there. "They were overcome when they saw him, and his mother said to him, 'My child, why have you done this to us?'" Isn't that how any mother would feel? She added, "See how worried your father and I have been, looking for you." And young Jesus replied, "Why were you looking for me? Did you not know that I must be in my Father's house?" Luke concludes, "But they did not understand what he meant."[47]

In the tradition of a holy man or woman who despises the things of the world and *hates* his own life, Francis turned away from his family as he turned toward God. He was following the words of Jesus in John's Gospel, chapter twelve: "Anyone who loves his life loses it, and anyone who hates his life in this world will keep it for eternal life."

REDEFINING FAMILY RELATIONSHIPS

For eight hundred years now, people have been drawn with curiosity toward the lives of Francis and Clare. We look on the personalities and intentions of the first Franciscans as one of those moments in the history of the Church when religion was fresh and vibrant. But both Francis's and Clare's religious lives were based upon a rejection of their families. What does all of this mean? Why would it be necessary to abandon one's earthly family for a spiritual one?

We must consider the monastic understanding of *conversion*. In the sixth century, St. Benedict of Nursia wrote in his *Rule* of the importance of undergoing what is called *a conversion of life*, a total renunciation of what is past in order to focus solely on what is godly. "Admission to the religious life should not be made easy," Benedict wrote, saying that only a man who keeps knocking at the front door, asking for entrance to the monastery (and to the life), should be admitted. Most men will go away after a short while of being ignored or rejected, and Benedict advises making one wait for several days! Then, once a man enters into the life, it is intended to be harsh and difficult, "won" (not earned) by great effort and determination. This includes turning away from everyone who had previously comforted or cared for the candidate. And then, "If he owns anything, he must either give it to the poor beforehand, or deed it to the monastery, keeping nothing for himself, for he owns nothing, not even his own body. When this is done he is to change his clothes for those of the community."[48] His old self is now dead and his converted self has begun.

By converting, Francis was turning away from the bondage of the world, which he believed to include his father and mother. The freedom of childhood had become for him (literally, at one point, at least) shackles and obstacles to true freedom in Christ. Francis had shown, up until that final, absolute break, how a repentant man can sometimes still be in chains. But he also showed that confession and contrition are sometimes not what is called for, but instead, complete and total conversion.

Sometimes, however, the language of monastic conversions can be overblown. Thomas of Celano describes the world that Clare left behind as "the filth of Babylon," a description that would be somewhat absurd if applied to her comfortable home and seemingly loving family. Clare's actions were similarly dramatic and bold, if somewhat less ostentatious. When she fled her family in the middle of the night and stealthily made her way to meet Francis and his group of friars at Portiuncula, Thomas of Celano alludes to a phrase from Hebrews 13; she moved "outside the camp," he said, describing Clare's leaving the safe and familiar for the unknown. Throughout the conversion narratives of both Francis and Clare, as well as in classic monastic texts such as Benedict's *Rule*, when saints leave their families behind, it is as if a soldier has gone off to fight.

When the men of Clare's family came for her, she refused to listen to their arguments and she would not allow herself to be removed. Imagine if your teenaged sister or daughter had run away from your family home and had gone to live with a group of men considered by most people to be lunatics. What would you have done? Would you have looked on your runaway sister or daughter as being well on her way to sainthood? Turning one's back on one's earthly parents was seen as necessary if it meant that one's identity could be fully realized in God. When Clare arrived at Portiuncula on that first night, in the words of one biographer, she "gave to the world her letter of divorce" as she took on the hair, clothes, and vows of a woman married to Christ.[49]

Clare advised others to make the same sort of distinctions in their lives when they were called to a religious life. Conversion was total. In one of her letters to Agnes of Prague, Clare calls her disciple Agnes the "daughter of the King of Kings" in contrast to her earthly state as daughter of the King of Bohemia, Ottokar I (d. 1230). Clare also rejoiced when Princess Agnes chose virginity over marriage. Why? Is there something wrong with marriage? No, but to Francis and Clare, a conversion that involved choosing virginity, like choosing poverty, was complete and permanent. Or, at least, it was more complete and permanent than are, for instance, decisions to sin less or to do good more often.

The ultimate beauty of a Franciscan life in the early days came through its proximity to replicating the life of Christ. Christ was poor—he owned nothing; and Christ was chaste—he never married. The physical hardships of poverty and virginity were exactly the point, for Francis and then Clare, of a converted life; they were twin aspects of true Gospel living.

They both intended to do nothing less than turn the world upside down. *Light in the Dark Ages* is a very broad claim for the title of this book, but it is true. Not that the medieval period was so dark, as the old textbooks used to claim; it was actually a tremendous time of faith and piety that we should admire in many ways. The label "Middle Ages" originated at the very beginning of the Renaissance in the late fifteenth century. Its purpose was to distinguish between the classical era of Greek and Roman civilizations, and the rediscovery of those classical forms in the emerging Renaissance. The creativity of Francis's and Clare's lives and movement was one of the most important markers in the time leading up to the color of the fourteenth and fifteenth centuries.

The wars, corruption, and disease that Francis and Clare faced were dark indeed. We most often imagine them with birds, and flowers, and rabbits, and calming wolves to rest by their sides, but we might just as well listen to them as prophets who sought an entirely different way of living.

They believed that any negative effects of conversion, such as leaving behind parents, are easily surpassed by the true freedom that comes from a total lack of attachments. Clare spoke at least for women when she declared in her first letter to Agnes that to be faithful and converted is to become "the bride, mother and sister of Jesus Christ." In Matthew 12, Jesus said, "Anyone who does the will of my Father in heaven is my brother and sister and mother." Clare added "bride" to the mix. Francis said that we are indeed all three of these at once, when we are fully converted. In what is referred to as the second version of "The Letter to the Faithful," Francis said that the Spirit of the Lord will dwell with those men and women who have persevered in faithfulness. Then, he described the various functions of those who take on new roles in the redefined family relationships that come with conversion:

> They are spouses, brothers, and mothers of our Lord Jesus Christ. *Spouses* when the faithful soul is united to Christ by the Holy Spirit. *Brothers* when we do the will of the Father. And *mothers* when we carry Christ in our hearts and bodies through love and a pure spirit, giving birth to Jesus through all holy activity, showing ourselves as an example to the world.

Clare and Francis wanted to live as they believed Jesus intended for people to live, with lives transformed by a reordering of what it means to be family—bride, mother, father, sister, and brother. Imagine a group of people who truly follow these teachings of Jesus and you will see how the first Franciscans lived with each other. The old claims of biological families—for marriages, children, inheritances, work, and commerce—no longer apply. One's father and mother may be not biologically but spiritually chosen. One's brothers and sisters are every person whom we meet.

Jesus turned the law of Moses on its head when he declared that our neighbors are those to whom we owe the most. The prophet Isaiah had foretold of that servant of Israel who would come and bring forth justice to the nations in this way. In chapter

42, Isaiah even extends our neighborly commitments to people whom most of us would never expect to care for. Similar to Francis and Clare and their care for lepers, imagine if we actually imitated Jesus to the point of doing what Isaiah said was to be done: "I have given you as a covenant to the people, a light to the nations, to open the eyes that are blind, to bring out the prisoners from the dungeon, from the prison those who sit in darkness." What would happen if Christians were to lead the way in opening the doors of prisons, inviting "those who sit in darkness" to come and sit among us; to advocate for early release programs for those who do not pose a threat to the community; to forgive them, reconcile with them, and embrace them as our brothers and sisters? What if more Christians were to do the same with lepers, and those modern-day lepers who suffer from diseases that are still vague, unknown, and dangerous? That is what Francis and Clare were doing, and it was turning the world upside down.

There was a time when Francis was staying at the Franciscan friary in Monte Casale, which was situated in a wilderness known for harboring thieves and dangerous men. One evening, three men who had become infamous in the area knocked on the door of the friary looking destitute and asking for food. The young friar who answered the door was known as Angel. Rather than invite the men in and feed them, Angel said to them, "You are not worthy to even walk on the earth, for you do not show reverence to humans or to God, who created you. Get out of here!" Francis rebuked Angel and forced him to run after the men with alms, while Francis prayed to God to soften the men's hearts. The hospitality shown that night led the three thieves to eventually become friars themselves.[50]

Our saints intended to redefine—as Jesus had before them—what it means to be a child, sister, brother, mother, and father. Jesus said to his parents in the temple at age twelve, "Why were you looking for me? Did you not know that I must be in my Father's house?" Later, in the Sermon on the Mount, Jesus' message included redefining who we are and to whom we are related. When the disciples were arguing before the Passion about which one of them was the greatest, Jesus said that children were the greatest. This was shocking to them! Our over-sentimentalizing of children and childhood today blurs our ability to see the scene clearly: in antiquity, children were of very little value to adults and viewed as incomplete human beings.

Just as the Apostle Paul later defined love in his first letter to the Corinthians, Jesus defined family and neighbor in ways that had never before been understood. Jesus said: You have heard that the Law says not to murder? I say: Do not be angry with your brother. Do not even insult your sister. Your sacrifices are ineffective if you have unresolved conflict with another person. You have heard that the Law says not to commit adultery? I say: Even the thoughts of your minds and the wishes of your imaginations betray you. You have heard that the Law says an eye for an eye and a tooth for a tooth? I say: Do not even resist someone who wants to do you harm. If someone wants to steal your coat, give him also your cloak. You have heard that the Law says you should love your neighbor and hate your enemy? I say: Love your enemies and pray for them, too. All people are your neighbors. All men are your brothers. All women are your sisters. Obey your Father in heaven. What Jesus was doing was very new, unusual, and full of reformation of what it means to be in relationship.

Francis and Clare restored nobility to the human being. This was one of their greatest gifts to their age. G. K. Chesterton wrote:

> Workhouses and lunatic asylums are thronged with men who believe in themselves. Of Francis it is far truer to say that the secret of his success was his profound belief in other people. . . . Francis always assumed that everyone must be just as anxious . . . as he was. He planned a visit to the Emperor to draw his attention to the needs of "his little sisters the larks." He used to talk to any thieves and robbers he met about their misfortune in being unable to give rein to their desire for holiness. It was an innocent habit, and doubtless the robbers often "got round him," as the phrase goes. Quite as often, however, they discovered that he had "got round" them, and discovered the other side, the side of secret nobility.[51]

We call Francis the saint of peace, but often forget that his caring was both personal and political. It was common for Francis to step into the middle of some political dispute between the wealthy and the unfortunate in Assisi in order to see that the poor's interests were represented properly. Francis believed that the sign of a person who has been transformed or is becoming transformed by the Spirit of God is peacefulness and carefulness in dealing with other people.

It can be difficult to relate to this aspect of Franciscan spirituality today. We have built up tremendous boundaries for ourselves, and between ourselves and others, don't-touch-me-or-invade-my-space boundaries. Francis did, too. He was wealthy and privileged—his father taught him to carry himself in such a way that that would be evident to all. That is why he deliberately made himself less sure, less confident in his appearance, or in the way in which he carried himself. In order to understand this spirit today, we would have to attend our next business meeting, church service, or society event by removing our shoes or untucking our shirts, or walking around touching strangers on the shoulder, or messing up our hair, doing something outside our normal, safe, physical boundaries. We would do these little, *foolish* things to ourselves and then pretend as if nothing was different.

According to Francis and Clare, our identities are not summarized by biology, ancestry, or socialization. We are like Nicodemus, who couldn't understand how this realignment of human relationships could possibly work. When Jesus told him that all things change when we are born of the Spirit, Nicodemus asked Jesus two questions that have forever pigeonholed him as some sort of a dunce: "How can anyone who is already old be born? Is it possible to go back into the womb again and be born?"

But Nicodemus wasn't a dunce. We are still asking these questions today when we continue to follow traditional ways of understanding family. Francis and Clare taught that we don't really know who Jesus is. He is in the hungry, the poor, the oppressed, and the dispossessed. What Jesus is today he may not be exactly tomorrow. The first Franciscans formed their life in this tradition—wanting to be Jesus in the changing, ever-challenging world.

CHAPTER
6

NO FROWNING
SAINTS

Francis was being watched while his conversion was underway. Unlike most of us, who undergo conversions that are private and mostly internal, Francis's was played out in the piazzas of Assisi. His neighbors watched as he began to leave his father's table and beg for his daily bread, work not in his father's shop but with his hands to rebuild fallen church buildings, learn to pray the liturgical hours without help from monk or monastery, leave the piazzas and their crowds behind and head off into the valleys of the surrounding countryside, and preach repentance to others, even as he was himself learning what that meant. They saw Francis transform from a high-spirited teenager to a melancholy soldier to a cheerful man with nothing.

An almost flamboyant sense of drama marks the earliest efforts of Francis to distinguish himself from worldly concerns, family constraints, and even spiritual norms. The scenes are familiar to those who have read any of the biographies of the saint. He returns from a local, warring conflict against Perugia in disgrace and shame, probably having deserted; he begins to hear the voice of God speaking to him from a crucifix in an abandoned church; he steals from his father in order to give to the needy; he faces his father's wrath and accusations in the public square in front of the bishop's home and not only returns the money to his father but also strips naked, offering *everything* to him that is rightly his; and he wanders off alone into the wilderness around Assisi, known only to lepers and robbers.

St. Francis Renounces His Worldly Goods

Denial of self was paramount to Francis in those early days. At first, he felt that he had so much to give up before he could honestly call himself a follower of Christ. Working with his hands, doing difficult work, was not only his obedience but also his penance.

A rich man of Assisi by the name of Bernard of Quintavalle was one of those observing Francis. He was intrigued by the younger man and respected his work around the city, saving abandoned churches and seeking to better the lives of others. But Bernard, being very successful, felt that he knew the qualities that would make a genuine leader rather than a charlatan. Bernard wanted to see the unkempt Francis up close and over a period of time. He invited him one night to his house.

Bernard asked Francis to have supper with him. Francis readily accepted, anxious to have a dedicated audience. One of the great historians of the Franciscan movement writes: "What took place within the walls of that house during that night has deeply affected the history of the Christian Church, for it was during those hours that the Order of Friars Minor was born."[52] While they ate together in Bernard's lovely home, we see none of the behavior that would later distinguish Francis from his wealthy hosts in similar situations. In later years when Francis was invited to eat with cardinals or lords, he would do things like beg for bread outside in the street while a sumptuous meal was being prepared for him and the others by servants inside, and he would return to the table with his meager scraps, insisting on eating only those. But that came later, in Francis's mature religious life, when he possessed a confidence that was absent from his early years.

Bernard asked Francis many questions about religion and Christian discipleship during their time together. They were there for a long time—so long, in fact, that Bernard eventually asked Francis to stay the night. Bernard knew that Francis's roof was often only the stars, and he had probably begun to take a real liking to the young man. *The Little Flowers* says that it was Bernard's "secret wish" from the beginning to test Francis's faith to the point of inviting him to spend the night, but that may be a later editor's interpretation. It turned out that the two men had many things in common.

So Bernard had a bed prepared for Francis in the same space in which he himself usually slept. Francis prepared himself for bed and got in, pretending to fall soundly asleep. Within a short while, Bernard too began to snore and, at that sound, Francis rose to pray. It turns out, however, that Bernard was the cleverer of the two, since he was also pretending to sleep, wanting to observe something of Francis's private life. As he continued his pretend snoring, what Bernard saw convinced him of his guest's unfeigned spirit. There was young Francis rocking slightly to and fro, praying over and over again as if he were searching deep inside himself for something. *Deus meus et omnia*: "My God and my all."

Soon after that evening, Bernard of Quintavalle became the first of Francis's disciples. Bernard and another man who was very successful in both law and Church, Peter of Catani, came to find Francis, probably while he was carrying rocks from Assisi down to San Damiano, asking how to join him in the work. This wasn't simply a case of two men wanting to carry some rocks or help out for a day. There was something about Francis's commitment and spirit that communicated a complete change of life. His was a life of thorough *conversion*. There was deep meaning in Francis's otherwise rudimentary work that struck others as profound and important.

At first, Francis was full of hesitancy, not really knowing how to take on followers. His first instincts were to be sure to do everything correctly. He knew that there were groups of mendicants and ascetics frequently wandering in Italy and France and elsewhere who were outside the boundaries of orthodox faith. Francis wanted to live the life correctly. Even in his later years, he would never become overconfident in his own instincts; he was always questioning himself.

Francis suggested that he, Bernard, and Peter go to the bishop's house in Assisi and open the Scriptures together for guidance. Once they arrived, the tradition tells us that Francis opened the Gospels randomly, searching for wisdom in that haphazard way that people do when they are at a loss for what comes next. Tradition says that they read three passages. First, Francis opened the book at random and probably asked one of the other men to read what his eyes first set upon. Bernard read Matthew 19:20–21.

> The young man said to [Jesus], "I have kept all [of the commandments]. What more do I need to do [to have eternal life]?" Jesus said, "If you wish to be perfect, go and sell your possessions and give the money to the poor, and you will have treasure in heaven; then come, follow me."

Francis picked up the book again, and leafing forward, searched quickly for another relevant passage. This time, he probably asked Peter to read what his eyes first landed on. It was from Luke 9:1–3:

> [Jesus] called the Twelve together and gave them power and authority over all devils and to cure diseases, and he sent them out to proclaim the kingdom of God and to heal. He said to them, "Take nothing for the journey: neither staff, nor haversack, nor bread, nor money; and do not have a spare tunic."

Finally, Francis may have read the last passage himself, turning back toward the beginning of the ornate book of Gospels that they had borrowed from the luxurious home of the bishop.

He returned to Matthew's Gospel, which would later become the one that he quoted more often than any other, and read from chapter 16, verses 24 and 25:

> Then Jesus said to his disciples, "If anyone wants to be a follower of mine, let him renounce himself and take up his cross and follow me. Anyone who wants to save his life will lose it; but anyone who loses his life for my sake will find it."

That was all that Francis, Bernard, and Peter required in order to create their first rule of life. The three quickly returned to their homes to help Bernard sell all that he owned. Both Bernard and Peter were highborn, but Bernard was rich. They carried money out to give to the people of Assisi, its hospitals, pilgrims, and various places of need. There are many stories of Francis, Bernard, and Peter standing in the piazza distributing Bernard's money to the poor. We can imagine the commotion that this must have caused in town, as people buzzed around, grabbing for goods and coins but also wondering how it all could have happened. When Bernard's valuables were brought forth, the people surely filled his hallways like bees entering and leaving a hive. This further commotion would have cemented the notion of Francis's insanity in the minds of some, while intriguing others.

When Francis had begun begging for his bread two years earlier, his father was horrified at the sight of it and disowned him publicly before the entire town. Not only did Francis beg alms in the piazzas, but Thomas of Celano tells us that at some point he also began "begging for leftovers door to door,"[53] something that would have surely embarrassed his family. Francis also began declaring that his bride was Lady Poverty, no doubt another subtle jab at his father's expectations for him. Every Umbrian father wanted a woman of high character, good family, and decent dowry for his son to marry; Francis had Lady Poverty instead. Finally, when Francis began leading Bernard and Peter into this new life, it was the greatest disgrace for Peter Bernardone. Now, Francis was leading other noble people to do the same. The very public nature of what was happening must have made his son's conversion all the harder to stomach for Peter Bernardone. But what brought shame to his father brought glory to Christ, Francis thought. The ways of God confound the wise, the reasonable, and the predictable.

Isn't it amazing that men were willing to follow a ragtag Francis on a mission when they had so much to lose? They wouldn't have done it if Francis was only one in a long line of dour and disapproving saints. People have always been attracted to Saints Francis and Clare because they seem to have come so close to that enigmatic command of Jesus to the first disciples: "Be perfect." However, neither of them became a saint through their writings, or by athletic acrobatics of self-denial. It was Teresa of Avila, a later saint, who once poked playfully at the *frowning saints* of Christian tradition, saying that she never wanted to become one. "O Lord, deliver us from sour-faced saints!" she used to say. Francis and Clare would have agreed. Early self-denial transformed in them into the sort of joy and freedom that characterizes those who have given up everything for good.

Joy Turns to Foolishness

Francis and his new brothers often took their message to the lively outdoor places that still characterize Umbrian towns. As one old travel guide explains: "Italian life has always had a gregarious, outdoor character; hence the importance of loggias and piazzas. No one here has patience to sit still indoors for long. Italian chairs of all periods are notoriously uncomfortable. There are more bars serving standing customers in a hurry to get outside again than *caffes* with tables and chairs. Almost the only thing Italians have patience for is a good talker. To this they are ready to listen for hours."[54] The work of rebuilding the Church happened in the piazzas and cafes of Assisi and surrounding towns as Francis and Clare drew others to join in the good work. There are many tales of the first Franciscans spreading the word of their new life in the open air. And by all accounts, Francis was always a good talker.

The early Franciscans became experts at the unpredictable. Within a few years of the conversion of Bernard and Peter, when they had all become as close as brothers, there was a time when Bernard began to spend many hours each day in quiet contemplation, away from the activities of the other friars. Bernard had, in fact, become seriously adept at meditation, so much so that his reputation for long periods of mystical communion with God had earned him a reputation outside the community of friars. He was known throughout the area as a man who communed with God.

But Francis did not approve of contemplation when it was practiced to the exclusion of all other forms of faithfulness. Francis remembered that first day, years earlier, in the bishop's home when the three of them had read from Luke's Gospel that Jesus called the first twelve disciples to do two things: "to proclaim the kingdom of God and to heal." What was good for Jesus and his disciples would also be good for Francis and his. So, Francis searched out Bernard one morning as Bernard was deep in his meditation and commanded him to leave his quietude and go to the nearest Assisi church and preach from his heart to the people. Bernard resisted. I am not a preacher, he said. For his disobedience, Francis commanded poor Bernard to go immediately and preach in the first church he could find—and in his underwear.

A short time elapsed after Bernard's faithful leaving to do as he was told before Francis said to himself, *Who am I, to send my faithful brother Bernard, one of the first people to believe in my mission and one of the most respected men of Assisi, to go and preach in his underwear!* Francis reproached himself and prepared himself to go and join Bernard, and the two men preached together—in their underwear! From that pulpit, Francis spoke eloquently of the vanity of fancy garments and their contrast with an eternity of God's love. It is said that many people were converted to following Christ on that day.

STRENGTHS AND WEAKNESSES

Saints are people who live and act with great certainty. They have discovered a freedom that eludes most of us during our lifetimes. By *giving away* possessions, status, and ego, Francis boiled the meaning of life down to what is most essential. This is what he intended when he described freedom in simplicity.

It is difficult for us to imagine today how important the Christian basilica was during barbaric times. There was often no other civilization other than what was within its walls. After the fall of Rome, the light of science and art was threatened with extinction, and the basilica had to supply an education for the people. Within its walls was the power to illuminate the mind and inspire the imagination.

It was deemed important that people should go forth from the basilica instructed and well satisfied, and that they should return there with joy—as to a place where they found truth and beauty. In order to satisfy this ideal, a church had to contain a complete theology and a complete sacred poem. This was the aim of those artists who covered the churches throughout Italy with mosaics, and not only the apse of their buildings, but also often the naves, the vestibule, and the frontal with the history of both Testaments amplified

It does a Christian no good, Francis understood, to *take back* or *hold onto* things; our false self reemerges and we lose a portion of God's freedom and happiness.

There were occasions in the life of Francis, however, when we see his false self reappearing. We should never make the mistake of thinking that he was perfect. For example, he seems to have always had trouble living in his father's shadow. There were times when Francis rebuked his brothers with such ferocity that we almost see the elder Bernardone, rather than the son. This happened most of all when friars wanted to own things that Francis felt were unnecessary. He would combat these desires in others with a spirit that was unlike him, as if he were once again arguing against his father. He could also be fierce in denying their wishes, and occasionally mean. Even *The Mirror of Perfection*, that loving collection of tales written by his closest companions, recounts that Francis could be ornery when discussing with a friar the idea of owning more than one tunic. "He used to bitterly accuse those who wanted good fabric for their tunic, finding fault with those who believed contrary to him, and would then sew rougher material into his own."[55]

The same sort of old or false self seems to have reappeared in the arduous process of taking control, and then losing control, of his own Order later in life. "[Francis] wanted to obey, not to command,"[56] explains one scholar. But we see Francis frustrated at those times when he was caught between the desire to hold power and authority in order to do good things with it, and the shame and disappointment he must have felt when the same was taken away from him.

by the legends of the saints and crowned by the visions of the Apocalypse. Nothing can equal the effect of that noble figure of Christ which stands out prominently on a background of gold, standing in the midst of an encircling heaven, having on His left and right saints who offer up their crowns to Him. Below may be seen the Lamb resting on the mountain from which issue the four streams, symbolic of the Four Evangelists. Twelve sheep emerge from the two towns of Jerusalem and Bethlehem, signifying the Christian host recruiting in the synagogue and among the Gentiles.

Finally, amid the details that ornament these works of art appear stags and doves, lilies and palms, all the symbols of Christian antiquity that have been preserved and interpreted by an uninterrupted tradition. And, to show in a striking manner that it was not intended to be a source of secret instruction reserved for the initiated, but to give to all the key of these illuminating pictures, they were accompanied by inscriptions. Verses could be read beneath each mosaic which explained its meaning, pointed a lesson, sought to move the spectator, and draw from him a tear or a prayer. These grand and austere walls, these Roman churches became like so many pages in which were celebrated the miracles of the saints, the princely founders of the basilica, and the famous dead sleeping beneath its roof.

—Frederick Ozanam

Again from *The Mirror of Perfection*, we at first see that Francis resigned the office of minister-general of the Order, appointing Peter Catani in his place: "Francis remained forever, from that time forward, a subject, bearing himself humbly in all things until his death, even more than all of the others." But two short chapters later, *The Mirror* recounts a conversation in which Francis tells one of his brothers the real reason why he resigned his office: he didn't feel that the friars were following his leadership. On his deathbed, he rose and cried out, "Who are those who would steal my Order and my brothers from my hands! When I come to General Chapter, I will show them who they are!"[57]

Francis and Clare lived with certainty when they were far away from power and authority. People who do great things usually act with little doubt, and both of our saints had confidence in their mature years, listening to the Spirit of God in their consciences. Mahatma Gandhi wrote in his autobiography: "I am far from claiming any finality or infallibility about my conclusions. One claim I do indeed make and it is this. For me they appear to be absolutely correct, and seem for the time being to be final. For if they were not, I should base no action on them."

In his *Testament*, Francis said, "No one showed me what I had to do, but the Most High himself revealed to me that I should live according to the pattern of the holy gospel." Clare pursued holiness so doggedly that she would, at times, challenge her superiors on matters of faith and practice. Most famously, Clare provided the first example of a hunger strike undertaken as a means of changing the status quo. After Francis's death, Pope Gregory worried about the Poor Clares being too much exposed to the influence of men—the friars—going in and out of the convent. The men would bring food and other goods to the women's monastery, and they would also come to preach and teach. Clare valued her brothers so much that she could not tolerate their being taken from her. So, she told the sisters to stop taking food and other things from the hands of the friars if they would not also be allowed by the minister-general to come into the enclosure and teach. The sisters would not eat if they could not also spend time with their brothers. When the minister-general reported the situation to Pope Gregory, he immediately reversed his decision.

She was undoubtedly tough. On another occasion, Clare challenged political and military powers in ways that were uncommon for a cloistered woman. One of the most famous episodes in Clare's life—reproduced in iconography of all kinds over the centuries—took place more than a decade after the death of Francis. It happened in September 1240 at San Damiano. Emperor Frederick II (who, ironically, had been betrothed as a younger man to Clare's disciple Agnes of Prague) was warring with the pope and hired Saracen mercenaries as part of his invading armies. They would hit and run, destroying their various targets, many of them religious foundations throughout the Italian city-states that were dear to the pope and also relatively unprotected. When these foreign fighters surrounded the monastery at San Damiano, while the other women very understandably hid somewhere inside undoubtedly praying fervently for their safety, Clare led a procession of one outside into the yard holding the Eucharist (or, Christ himself) before her, "striking" at the men with its power. In the paintings of this scene, Clare is usually depicted as holding high a monstrance that contained the Eucharistic host. Scholars know that the monstrance was not actually created until sometime after the Council of Trent in the sixteenth century, but nevertheless, the message is clear: Clare used Christ as her instrument in battle. In this instance, Clare also shows herself to have been powerful in a way that Francis was not.

But just as Francis and Clare were both charismatic leaders, they were not organizers. They also were not good administrators. They were too busy to worry about the future, and they felt too free to spend much time brooding over ideas, something that would have tied them down to libraries, desks, and books. Their leadership was high on charisma and low on follow-through. To take even a small detail, for example, the only gardening that we know of Francis and Clare doing was flowers, to show the beauty of creation. They saw no point to sowing seeds that would one day in the future feed them. Miguel de Unamuno echoed Francis and Clare a century ago when he wrote, "There is no future; there never is any future. What is known as the future is one of the greatest of lies."[58] Today is always what mattered, what was real.

Francis and Clare's convictions were so ideal as to confound worldly realities. They refused to even handle money, or to take possession of any single thing. They felt free to borrow shelter or space or things, but never to have things as their own. They wanted to follow Christ, whom they saw as a stranger and a homeless man. So, for instance, if Francis had been given a large sum of money in order to fund a chain of leper hospitals across Europe, he probably would have turned it down.

Francis's and Clare's personalities were such that they were most free when they were following a simple path of living by a *Rule* and listening to the Spirit. Does this mean that they failed to leave the world with meaningful change and permanent reform? Perhaps in some sense, it does. They did not build hospitals, orphanages, or schools; they did not create foundations or fund philanthropies that would outlive them. Their work was of a much more personal nature. The influence of the dynamic is more difficult to characterize than is the influence of those who organize and administer.

The lives of Francis, Clare, and the first Franciscans were marked by charity and compassion that does not compare with the sort of work that is done by large organizations. They did not want their movement to be yet another career path for social advancement and power in the Church. They wanted only simple and joyful men and women. They always believed themselves called to a life of following Christ, and they cut away anything that stood in the way. They were not as interested in changing institutions as they were in impacting individual lives. They cared for people immediately, rather than caring for their needs longer term. But the sheer numbers of Franciscans in the first decades had an enormous impact on the world, and after the passing of Francis and Clare, those friars and sisters began to do some of those things that the founders had avoided. Francis, Bernard, and Peter began the movement in 1209, and by 1250, there were about thirty thousand men and women. Hundreds of Franciscan friaries existed within a decade of Francis's death, and a thousand by 1275.

Their legacy is full of extraordinary strengths and also basic weaknesses. Within a few years of receiving his first followers, Francis became known throughout Assisi for his simple greeting: "Peace and all good"—or, in Italian, "*Pace e Bene!*" During his lifetime, that was the purpose of his daily life, nothing more and nothing less. Clay plaques all over Assisi proclaim the same today.

TRYING TO BE LIKE JESUS

T he procession through town each Palm Sunday morning in Assisi involved nearly every citizen. Small chapels and businesses were closed on that important day so that all could be present for the march into the city center, the hearing of the complete Passion sung from the Gospel of Matthew, and most of all, the general communion.[59] The populace gathered outside the city walls with branches and flowers in hand, waiting for the procession to begin. The walls of medieval cities in Italy and elsewhere made it possible to reenact the first procession of Jesus into Jerusalem with a certain degree of accuracy. The people of Assisi were reminded, both by the words of their bishop and also by the symbolism of the march through the city gates, that this was as Jesus had entered the city of Jerusalem for the last time.

There was a heightened drama given to the reading of the Passion. A melodious Italian baritone would recite the words of Christ, while a deliberately harsh male voice would call out the chants from the crowd and the words of the disciple who betrayed him. It was this sort of dramatic rendering of the Passion that allowed the uneducated to understand what was happening, despite the use of a Latin text.

All of highborn Assisi was there on Palm Sunday morning, March 18, 1212. The day stood symbolically between the activities of the Lenten season and the business of Holy Week. The Saturday before Palm Sunday was the occasion for the last preparations of the boy and girl catechumens. The catechumens were all young children, much younger than Clare was in 1212. The rituals of preparation included breathing on the children, chanting Gospel verses above their heads, and anointing each child as set apart from the world, for Christ. One week later, on Holy Saturday, the neophytes would all be baptized formally into the Church.

At the conclusion of Mass on Palm Sunday, it was customary for each girl of marriage age to personally greet the bishop, presenting herself to him in a manner befitting a lady. For most of the girls in town, this event represented a high point in the year and was worried over, and prepared for, for weeks. It was a prelude of their marriage ceremonies to come, when all eyes were on the bride processing glamorously and joyfully down the aisle, back then just as now.

As we have already seen, Clare distinguished herself from all of the other girls by refusing to show herself as an eligible woman on that day. As all of refined Assisi watched, Clare refused to stand to greet the bishop, something that all of the young women did in order to receive his blessing and to show themselves to the rest of the town. Thomas of Celano tells us that it was Francis who instructed Clare in how to play along with the drama of the Palm Sunday routine. He even told her to dress in her finest clothes and to go forward with the other girls to receive her palm frond from the bishop, according to Thomas. It seems possible, however, that it was Clare herself who decided not to participate. If Francis had declared his marriage to Lady Poverty, Clare could also find another spouse. Her religious life began on that day.

THE ART OF SPIRITUAL IMITATION

Faithful to the principles of hagiography, Clare's spiritual life was said to have actually begun before she was born. It seemed to the medieval imagination that, if Clare did the great things that she did in life, she must also have been remarkable before birth and after death. That is how saints were once *made* in the pages of hagiography.

The very first story told of Clare's spiritual life is, in fact, modeled on the Gospel accounts of the Annunciation to the Virgin Mary. Like the Virgin Mother, Clare's mother was said to have experienced a divine intervention with regard to a pregnancy. While already pregnant with Clare, her mother Ortolana was praying in the church of San Rufinus begging for mercy and comfort in childbirth when a voice from God said, "Woman, do not be afraid, for you will give safe birth to a child whose light will illuminate the world." This is why Ortolana named her Clare, which literally means *light*.

This sort of imitation of saints from the past was common practice in the composing of a new saint's legends. Christians inherited this sort of imitation from Judaism, where important figures such as Moses, Isaiah, and Jonah became types of people who would come later. The Gospels tell many stories, such as the feeding of the five thousand, in a way that show Jesus as the *new*

Moses. The first recorded Christian martyr, St. Stephen, summarized this understanding in the eloquent sermon he preached before the high priest, recorded in Acts 7. Stephen compared Jesus to Moses in that both were powerful in words and deeds, sent by God to rescue his people, rejected by those same people, but then returned to free them from bondage.

As Jesus was the new Moses, so, too, did Jesus tell his followers to *follow* him. St. Paul later said the same, "Be imitators of me, as I am of Christ."[60] And so on it goes, as Christians have ever since sought to model themselves on those who have gone before. The hagiographer who models a saint's life by interpreting it through this sort of lens is doing something perfectly legitimate. Francis and Clare modeled their lives after Jesus and the Virgin Mary, and so did the first Franciscans model their lives after Francis and Clare. Being *Franciscan* was, after all, the whole purpose of becoming a friar or a sister—to become like Francis and Clare.

Unlike some other saints, however, Francis and Clare became renowned for their exact attention to detail in following Christ. They were imitators to a remarkable degree, seeking to eat as Jesus ate, sleep as he slept, travel as he traveled, and to do and not do what the Gospels tell us that Jesus did and didn't do. After Francis's death, Clare praised him in her *Testament* by saying that he was an imitator of Christ to the point of following in Christ's very footprints. Today, we read something like this with a spiritualizing eye, but it was not originally intended that way. The distance of twelve hundred years meant nothing to Francis and Clare; they modeled their apostolic lives as if Jesus was their contemporary.

The Mirror of Perfection provides some interesting detail of these measures taken by Francis. Here are some of the occasions in his life when he consciously did as his master had done down to the smallest, seemingly insignificant, details.

Chapter of Mirror[61]	Example of imitating Christ	References to the words of Christ
3	Refusing to own even spiritual books, as an expression of complete poverty.	"Take nothing for the journey: neither staff, nor haversack, nor bread, nor money; and do not have a spare tunic." (Luke 9:3)
4	Teaching the dangers of arrogance in learning to a novice who wanted to pursue studies.	"To you is granted to understand the secrets of the kingdom of God; for the rest it remains in parables." (Luke 8:10)
9	Refusing to stay in a cell if it was said to be his.	"Foxes have holes and the birds of the air have nests, but the Son of Man has nowhere to lay his head." (Matthew 8:20)
19	Instructing cooks in the communities not to prepare food the night before it was to be eaten.	"So do not worry about tomorrow." (Matthew 6:34)

A French writer has called this attention to mimicking the life of Jesus "naïve, almost manic imitation."[62] Another, more positive spin explains that Francis was both unaware of more complex ways of reading the Scriptures and uninterested in discovering them: "The son of a prosperous merchant who had passed his youth in irresponsible and extravagant gaiety, he was ignorant of the theological commentaries on the words that might have slurred over their challenge, and he accepted, impulsively and with joy, their literal, practical application."[63] There are many additional examples from Francis's life and writings as well. For instance, in his *Later Rule*, Francis instructed all of his brothers to not only preach in language that is well chosen and chaste, but to always preach with brevity: "because our Lord kept his words brief while on earth." Bringing healing comfort to lepers was an imitation of Jesus, who healed ten lepers in Luke 17.

Francis's rebuilding of San Damiano was his first act of spiritual literalism. He was always one to do precisely what was asked, spending relatively little time trying to discern more subtle meanings to what he felt God had said directly to him. "Go and rebuild my church" was what the figure on the crucifix said as he knelt before it seeking meaning for his life. And so, literally, Francis rebuilt the Church by first rebuilding churches. Francis would not have gained the followers that he did if he had not been literal in his commitments. It was precisely his idealism that drew people to join him. There is simple beauty and attraction in doing what needs to be done regardless of other consequences.

There is an art to spiritual imitation, and it isn't only done through the physical details of life. Søren Kierkegaard taught that faith is impossible without a personal, passionate inwardness that takes hold of one's life. Each person's passion will be individual, but never unique, if it is truly formed around the God to whom we focus all of our attention. Trying to be like the great saints that have come before us is part of Christian discipleship. Imitation of Jesus is more important than praying to him—more important, even, than holding certain beliefs about him. As Simone Weil once argued in a letter to a priest, "Christ does not save all those who say to

Him: 'Lord, Lord.' But he saves all those who out of a pure heart give a piece of bread to a starving man, without thinking about Him the least little bit."[64]

A simple joy attached itself to the early Franciscans, as friars and then sisters attempted to follow Christ's commands to the letter, asking very few questions that might fill a modern mind with doubts. Their love for obeying gave birth to a special sort of knowledge. As Jesus praised children for their simple faith, it is this same sort of deliberate simplicity that filled Francis and Clare with a knowledge of God in the soul that is quite different from any book knowledge. For whatever reasons, they could not have made a personal synthesis of the two—firsthand faith and book knowledge—as Thomas Aquinas or Bonaventure later did. Francis and Clare's commitments were Gospel-literal. In many ways, one might say that they followed Christ in every detail, except for when Christ went into the temple where discussions of ideas take place.

THE TROUBLE WITH LEARNING

Their movement assumed that Scripture study and theology were of little value to a friar or sister. A true man of God would not want or need such things, Francis believed, for the Gospels would be sufficient. Due to the absence of formal theological study and teaching, we may assume that the early friars held and tolerated a wide variety of opinion on such matters. Silence breeds imagination. But Francis had no time for speculation of any kind. He was a man of action and believed that academic study could make it so that a person no longer sees the rest of the world clearly—as the librarians in Jorge Luis Borges's story "The

"All knowledge," said the holy doctor, Bonaventure, "is contained in two books. The one, inspired from within, embodies all the divine ideas—the prototypes of all the substances to which they have given birth. The other book, inspired from without, is the world in which the thoughts of God are imprinted in imperfect and perishable characters. The angel reads from the first, the beast from the second. Creation was imperfect while it lacked a being who could read in both books at once, and who could interpret the one by the other. That is our destiny, and philosophy has no other use than that of leading us to God by all branches of creation."

No one spoke the language of symbolism more boldly than St. Bonaventure in his all too little-known pamphlets. The very titles of these would be appropriate for hymns and dithyrambs: *The Six Wings of the Seraphim, The Seven Roads of Eternity, The Journey of the Soul to God*. The good doctor

Secret Miracle," who went blind looking for God among 400,000 volumes. It was as if Francis said to his followers: "Follow me, following Christ. Do as I do. Work, preach, practice charity; don't own, worry, or look to the future; and believe as you will."

Francis believed that, parti-cularly among those men who are drawn to full-time religious life, learning can often substitute for, rather than support, spiritual practice. He probably knew the famous sermons of Bernard of Clairvaux on the Song of Songs that included Bernard's opening statement about the passionate, firsthand experience necessary to understand the mysteries of God: "Only the touch of the Spirit can inspire a song like this, and only personal experience can unfold its meaning. Those who are versed in the mystery may revel in it. All others should burn with desire to attain to this experience rather than settle for merely learning about it."[65]

When talking with a young friar who wanted to own books for himself, Francis once used an analogy that explained his position most clearly: There are great soldiers who have fought in heroic battles, and they are usually followed by other men who desire only to tell the stories of the soldiers' valor, rather than duplicate the heroic deeds in their own lives. Similarly, Francis explained, there are those who live in spiritual practice and deepening faith, and then there are those who desire only to read about such possibilities.

On another occasion, Francis accepted some students of canon law who wanted to become friars, but in their cases, part of forsaking the world according to the *Rule* was to leave behind their studies. This happened in

knew that it was not mere intelligence that would help us to recognize the eternal beauty that hides itself behind the veil of nature. In order to elude what despoils it, in order to pursue it—we must also have love. Love is the foundation of that wisdom that trusts less to syllogism than to prayer.

Love is also the culmination of wisdom, for do not imagine that Bonaventure would have been satisfied with the barren knowledge of the Creator and His attributes. Having arrived at the point where reason fails, he burned with a desire to penetrate further. He wished, he says, to lay aside the powers of reason for a time and to direct all his understanding and being towards God until his will might be merged in God's. But, when asked by what means that would be possible, Bonaventure urged the necessity of grace and not knowledge, desire and not thought, prayer and lamentations and not the study of books, the spouse and not the master, God and not humanity.

"Let us die then to ourselves," he continued. "Let us enter into the mysteries of the darkness. Let us impose silence on solicitude, on desire, on the phantoms of the senses, and, in the train of the Christ crucified, let us pass from this world to our Father."

—Frederick Ozanam

Bologna, and the men's names were Pellegrino and Rinieri. Francis instructed Pellegrino "to follow the way of humility in the Order" by not using his learning or even becoming a priest. He asked the young student to be a humble lay brother. Rinieri, meanwhile, became the minister to the friars of the region known as the Marches of Ancona, a place that will feature prominently later on in our story.[66]

On still another occasion, Francis taught his brothers that even if an eminent cleric were to join the movement, Francis would want him to renounce his learning at least to some degree, as learning itself is a form of riches. Revealingly, the man who came to be known as the Poverello, or *little poor man*, explains: "Learning makes a man difficult to teach. One needs to be able to take something rigid, such as the expectations of Christ, and bend it into oneself through humble disciplines."[67] This sounds a lot like the camel going through the eye of a needle, but not quite so difficult as that.

In place of book learning, a life of simplicity was supposed to involve a keen connection to the earth, creatures, and humans, in ways that were unlike those of saints before them. In a very real sense, the generation led by Francis and Clare was the one that brought heaven and earth much closer than they had been since the days that Jesus was walking around in

Palestine. Before Francis, it was unheard of for a saint to speak of specific species rather than a more abstract creation, or to turn to creatures for understanding, rather than to God alone. Francis and Clare brought the earthly and the spiritual much closer together. They saw the world simply and differently from most of the other people around them. The earth was full of God in ways that books could not be. "There lives the dearest freshness deep down things . . . / Because the Holy Ghost over the bent / World broods with warm breast and with ah! / bright wings" (Gerard Manley Hopkins, from "God's Grandeur").

Nevertheless, the Franciscan movement began at "a significant juncture in the evolution of medieval theology: at a moment of intellectual, ecclesial, and spiritual ferment."[68] It was ironically Francis's charisma that attracted some of the brightest minds of the day to his way of life, and after the deaths of Francis and Clare, the life of the mind would become more important within the movement.

Had he lived to see it, it is tempting to imagine that Francis might have appreciated the way that Bonaventure was able to synthesize book learning with a firsthand experience of God. At the time of Clare's death in 1253, Bonaventure was already the most important theologian among the earliest Franciscans, and four years later he became their minister-general. Bonaventure was anxious to quiet the founders' anti-intellectual impulses. He himself came to be known by the glorious title "Seraphic Doctor," referring to his angelic character mixed with a rigorous mind. Like his Dominican contemporary Thomas Aquinas, Bonaventure was comfortable following Jesus into the temple. At the beginning of his *Life of St. Francis*, he calls Francis a "professor of evangelical perfection"—an accurate phrasing that nevertheless shows Bonaventure's love of learning as well as the saint's seriousness for the imitation of Christ.

JUGGLERS FOR GOD

Scholars have debated for centuries whether or not Francis or the bishop knew beforehand that Clare was coming to Portiuncula. Although there are traditions that say certain friars hurried her through the narrow streets of Assisi, and that the friars stood in the plain near Portiuncula with torches in their hands to beckon her coming, it is just as likely that she was completely alone that first night.

The structure of Portiuncula—which was known at that time by its religious name, *Santa Maria degli Angeli* (St. Mary of the Angels)—was built in the early Middle Ages, and there is a legend that it was originally intended to surround relics of the Virgin brought to Umbria from the Holy Land. The chapel was owned by the Benedictine monks of Monte Subasio. In 1211, the abbot gave Francis permanent use of it, and Francis gathered the friars together in small and temporary dwellings around it.[69] Their lives centered around the small altar inside the chapel throughout the day when they were not out working and preaching.

Many scholars have supposed that Portiuncula was the chapel that Francis repaired when he had finished at San Damiano. No place was more special to St. Francis; *Portiuncula* means "little portion of earth," a name that Francis gave to the place, and he would later die within its walls. It still stands today as a lovely medieval jewel surrounded by a much-less-attractive modern church known as the Basilica of St. Mary of the Angels. This is usually the first stop for pilgrims arriving in Assisi, as the basilica is within one hundred paces of the train station. Just outside the basilica, beside the first souvenir stalls, the buses stop to carry people for the short journey up into Assisi itself.

To walk briskly from Clare's family home to Portiuncula would take at least thirty minutes. That was a long time to have to worry, or to look over her shoulder for pursuers. Surely she knew that her actions would not only infuriate her family, but could put Francis at personal risk. Italian law called for financial and other penalties against men who married women without their family's consent. Any romantic such as Francis would have known this and would also have seen how Clare's coming to Portiuncula could be wrongly perceived. By all indications, though, Clare was not preoccupied but rather determined in her flight that night.

She surely had family running after her as soon as she was found missing. Perhaps that is why Francis cut Clare's hair that first night. Her golden curls can still be seen as one of the relics at the Basilica of Santa Clara in Assisi today. Francis made her a *sister* without any semblance of deliberation whatsoever. Afterwards, still within hours of her coming, she was bundled away to the Church of San Paolo at Bastia, part of a Benedictine monastery a few miles from Assisi. It is there that her family first accosted her, trying to convince her to return home, and then, a few days later, attempting to remove her forcibly.

A few days after arriving at San Paolo, Francis arranged to move Clare to the Benedictine convent of San Angelo, on the slopes of Assisi's Mount Subasio, where she was promised more protection and quiet. Sixteen days after her initial flight, Clare's sister Catherine, soon to be called Sister Agnes, joined her there. The two of them would have been viewed as runaways by many Assisans, and religious fanatics by most of the rest. Their parents and family members became determined again to convince the young women to return. This time, though, they focused on Catherine, physically dragging her away down the hillside until she was almost unconscious. It appears that Clare finally begged them to leave, appealing to what affection they might still feel for their daughter and sister, who was dying at their hands, determined to enter the religious life. It is uncertain exactly how long Clare and Catherine then stayed at San Angelo. They were joined by at least one other woman during that time, namely, their aunt, Pacifica, who was about twice their age. Together, the three of them formed a unique sort of family and were eventually moved into San Damiano after Francis begged the Benedictines and the bishop of Assisi (the same man who gave Francis his cloak when Francis disrobed before his father) for permission to use the church.

Is it only by accident that Francis arranged for Clare to live at San Damiano, where he had first heard so clearly the word of God? I don't think so. He must have hoped and expected that Clare would listen for that guiding voice just as he had.[70] A community quickly grew up around Clare to match the friars surrounding Francis. The sixteenth-century Franciscan historian Luke Wadding offers in his *Annales* the names of fifty women who comprised the convent at San Damiano by 1238. After Clare, Catherine, and Pacifica, the next sisters (later to be called *Poor Clares*) included Benvenuta, Cecilia, Amata (Clare's niece),

Christina (a childhood friend of Clare's), and Philippa—all names that figure prominently in Clare's religious life and in the growth of the Second Order. Clare's own mother, Ortolana, joined her daughter at San Damiano within a few years. Legend has it that she waited until after the death of her husband but then sold all of her possessions and distributed the money to the poor—just as Francis instructed and Brother Bernard had done. Ortolana arranged for her brother-in-law to care for Clare's younger sister, Beatrice, and was invested by Francis himself. Beatrice later joined the Poor Clares herself upon reaching the age of eighteen.

Precedents for the Poor Clares

It was the rare mother or father of the thirteenth century who desired their daughter to enter religious life rather than marry. As one medievalist has summarized, "Marriage was not only a sacramental act, it was a civic act. . . . Its rituals laid the foundation of the civic order."[71] In fact, given the corruption in the Church in Clare's day, it would be safe to say that in 1212, no one was encouraging young women to consider the religious life—especially intelligent and attractive young women. And to join Francis was not even as promising as joining a convent. To join Francis was the sort of action that would rightly terrify any parent.

The tradition of religious women was well established long before Francis and Clare. St. Paul instructs Timothy to honor widows, an ancient Jewish practice, but he also speaks of "the real widow, left alone, [who] has set her hope on God and continues in supplications and prayers night and day."[72] In the same letter, plus in his first letter to the church in Corinth,

Paul praises women who are virgins, urging them to practice devotion to God's work in lieu of passion to a husband.

Less than three hundred years after Paul's ministry, St. Pachomius (d. 346), one of the founders of monasticism, built a convent for religious women. St. Jerome (d. 420), too, urged both men and women to consider religious life as an antidote to the lax practices and corruption that he already detected in the secular, or non-monastic, clergy. Jerome would found a convent in Bethlehem with St. Paula (d. 404), the patron saint of widows, one of several prominent widows whom he mentored. Jerome spent most of the last three decades of his life working in that abbey, translating the Scriptures and writing his famous biblical commentaries.

Reform movements were necessary also in the centuries leading up to Francis and Clare. The first Cistercian monastery for women was established in what is now Dijon, France, in 1125. St. Dominic founded a convent of nuns only five and a half years before Clare fled to join Francis at Portiuncula. Having seen a vision of the Virgin Mary on the feast of St. Mary Magdalene in July 1206, Dominic understood from her that he was to establish a convent at Prouille, France, where he was busy trying to convert a heretical group known as the Albigensians. Before the end of December that year, the first Dominican convent had opened and was named for St. Mary Magdalene, who still at that time was identified with the penitent prostitute from the Gospels—in other words, a repentant, changed, and committed woman.

And so, when Clare fled to join Francis and his band of friars late that night, her actions were not exactly unprecedented, but they *were* unusual. There was no women's house for her to join. Where would she sleep? What sort of religious work would she do? Would Clare join the men during the day, working with them side by side? Some scholars suggest that this is indeed what happened in the first weeks of Clare's and Catherine's joining the movement. The earliest biographers tell a different story. Regardless, there was a recklessness in both Clare and Francis on that first night. They were fools, just as Christ had been a fool on the Cross. What G. K. Chesterton explains about Francis was also true of Clare:

> The conversion of St. Francis . . . involved his being in some sense flung suddenly from a horse. . . . [T]here was not a rag of him left that was not ridiculous. Everybody knew that at the best he had made a fool of himself. . . . [T]he word fool itself began to shine and change.[73]

Faith became playful in the expression of early Franciscanism. When the Church was beset by corruption and irrelevance, and kingdoms and local governments were more concerned with military conquest than with caring for citizens, the best spiritual response often included playfulness. Sometimes we need a remedy for malaise and trouble that resembles foolishness.

Francis called himself and his brothers *Jongleurs de Dieu* in French, or "God's Jugglers," because they were often the jovial men who would sing and dance with the people. They didn't always have to preach. In her intriguing book *What the Body Wants*, Cynthia Winton-Henry says, "Play is honest. You can't play unless you are yourself." After his conversion, Francis came to understand who he really was, and then he was able to be playful.

Francis was a poet and singer of songs, singing of the joy and cheerfulness in Gospel living and poverty. Three hundred years after his death, a Florentine historian made reference to "praise songs in Italian to the Sisters of Santa Clara" written by St. Francis that sadly are no longer extant, a fact that has depressed Franciscan scholars ever since.[74] The only Italian song of Francis that is still known to us today is the remarkable *Canticle of the Creatures*, which we will look at in detail in a later chapter. In their cheery approach to faith, Francis and Clare believed that they were provided another antidote to the gloom of their era, but also, they were imitating the joy of the first Christian communities.

In various collections of Italian verse, Francis of Assisi's *Canticle* is presented as the very first vernacular Italian poem. Francis's ministry took place at the beginning of the vernacular movement in Europe, both in the church and in literature. The Lateran Council of 1215 (almost ten years before the *Canticle* was written) said that all Christians had to recite certain core prayers such as the Our Father and Ave Maria in their own language, rather than in Latin, by confirmation age.[75] Francis's creativity was a part of the ferment of his age in preaching and speaking in the vernacular. What really set him apart was his composing new work in Italian.

Strategic Foolishness

The early Franciscans reached into new communities, as well, by playing the fool. The texts tell us that Francis and Clare "desired to bear shame and insult for the love of Christ" and that "they traveled the world as strangers and pilgrims."[76] They were also smart enough to realize that this sort of life and approach would attract more people to their cause and movement.

The spiritual genius of Italian poetry developed in the atmosphere of the catacombs. We must descend there in order to discover the source of what was destined to come later. There, in those early days, lived a people in the modern sense of the word, comprising women and children, the weak and the small, such as ancient historians despise and hold of no account—a new people, a medley of strangers, slaves, free, barbarians, all animated by a spirit alien to the rest of antiquity wand suggestive of a new order of things.

This society had an ideal that it was eager to express, but the ideal was too comprehensive, too impassioned, too new, to find adequate expression in words. It required the service of all of the arts. In that early stage of its development, poetry was unclear and imprecise, but it animated all of the arts including architecture, painting, sculpture, and engraving. All of these are symbolic and characterized by figurative expression and the

Francis seems to have known that others would be drawn to a life of joy and simplicity. He once sent Brother Bernard to the nearby town of Bologna to begin the Franciscan movement there, preaching the good news of their way of rediscovering the life of Christ. Bernard's strategy was one of simple humility and foolishness. He walked into the city in his ragged robes (the Franciscans were known for the ugliest of monastic garments), and he sat in the city center reading the recently written *Rule* of St. Francis quietly to himself. Bernard stood out among the crowd of people in the square. He was poorly dressed, smiling at passersby, and was reading to himself in public—something that people rarely ever did in those days. Children began to mock him, thinking that he was a local idiot. In the Middle Ages, children could be even crueler than they are today, and they threw stones and mud at Bernard, calling him names. But Bernard only smiled, and greeted them with the love of Christ.

Some adults joined in mocking the friar while others curiously watched. Day after day Bernard came and went to the public square of Bologna doing these things until finally someone approached him, a lawyer who was impressed by his spirit and humility, and asked him what he was reading. Within days there were followers of Francis in Bologna. It is said that Francis "gave thanks to the Lord and then began to scatter his poor disciples of the Cross more widely . . . and many communities were established in many places."[77]

True joy will have subtle effects on one's environment. The effects of song, jocularity, human touch, and sharing goods among members of a community not only lower

attempt to make the image reflect the idea, to reveal the ideal in the real.

Imagine the catacombs: A network of long, underground corridors, stretching in all directions beneath the suburbs and outskirts of Rome. Do not confuse them with the spacious quarries dug out for the purpose of building the pagan city. The Christians themselves excavated the narrow corridors which were to hide the mysteries of their faith and to be the resting-places for their tombs. These labyrinths are sometimes as much as three or four stories high and they penetrate to a depth of eighty to one hundred feet below ground, but in many parts they are so narrow and low that it is difficult to make one's way through even with lowered head. To the right and left are several rows of broad, deep trenches scooped out of the wall, in which bodies of men, women, and children were once placed side by side. As if to confuse the pagan searchers, the underground passage makes a thousand detours, and to this day these very detours speak of the horrors of those early days of persecution when the cruel hunter chased his prey through these winding labyrinths.

No building raised by human hands teaches nobler lessons than the catacombs. In those murky passages the visible world and all trace of light is denied to all who penetrate those depths. The cemetery encloses all the hidden treasures of darkness, and the oratories, built at various points for the celebration of the holy mysteries, are like daylight breaking in upon immortality to comfort the souls for the night below.

These oratories are covered with pictures that are often crudely executed and that are clearly the work of unskilled hands. Yet often when the light of a torch is thrown upon the sacred walls, images are revealed whose design, form, and movement recall the best traditions of ancient art. Also, behind this simple art lurks a principle that was destined

blood pressures and increase life expectancies, but they blow fresh air and optimism all around. We cannot over-estimate the power that joy played in fueling the growth of the Franciscan movement. It is these intangibles that best explain why thousands upon thousands joined the two founders, and then why things also floundered, years later, in their absences.

There are deeper aspects to early Franciscan foolishness, as well. They not only played the fool, something that is already difficult enough to understand in our modern idiom, but they humiliated themselves. Francis would often ask his friars to step on his face, for instance, or to verbally remind him of his lowliness, as measures against pride. He sought to imitate Christ crucified, who allowed himself to be debased, mocked, and utterly without hope in the minds of others. Francis and Clare each also desired to be martyred like Christ, desires that would always go unrequited.

Just like juggling for God in the piazzas, all manners of foolishness were aimed at teaching spiritual lessons. For example, one should never be too reliant upon financial and material resources. Francis believed that all Christians should follow the teaching of Jesus not to worry about tomorrow, sharing with others who are in need. For this reason, when Francis went out to beg alms before sitting down to dine at the bishop of Ostia's house, he wasn't just being eccentric—he was challenging the structure of wealth and want. When he asked his brothers not to own personal prayer books, he wasn't just being literal in his pursuit of poverty—he was setting himself apart from the joint and institutional wealth of the monasteries of his day. All of these were aspects

to animate and transform it: The true faith of the martyrs is depicted in the expression of these beings represented by those early artists with eyes raised to heaven and hands outstretched in prayer. We discover, in these desolate places, a very different spirit.

At the entrance to a vault appears the Good Shepherd bearing on his shoulders a lamb and a goat, indicating that he saves both the innocent and the repentant. In four panels decorated with garlands of flowers and fruits, we see stories drawn from the Old and New Testaments, arranged in couples, as if to suggest allegory and reality, prophecy and history. We see Noah and the Ark, Moses striking the rock, Job on the dunghill, the Miracle of Cana, the feeding of the five thousand, Lazarus leaving the tomb, and most prominent—Daniel in the lions' den, Jonah cast out by the whale, the three Children in the furnace. We see no traces of contemporary persecutions, no representations of the butchering of the Christians, nothing bloodthirsty, nothing that could rouse hatred or vengeance, nothing but pictures of pardon, hope, and love.

Christian sculpture also had its beginnings here, and figures may be found that are roughly hewn, without proportion, without grace, with no other worth than the ideal that they represent. A leaf expresses the instability of life; a sailing boat, the fleeting of our days; the dove bearing the branch proclaims the dawn of a better world; the fish recalls baptism, and, at the same time, the Greek word which translates it unites in a mysterious anagram the majestic titles of the Son of God, the Savior. On one nameless tomb there is a fish and the five miraculous loaves of bread, suggesting that here rests a man who believed in Christ, who was regenerated by baptism, and who partook of the eucharistic feast.

As paganism gradually declined, the chisel of the Christian became bold and more productive. Instead of those indefinite emblems that

of conversion, according to Francis and Clare. They taught that there are many things, tendencies, and sins that we all must turn away from, in order to see and experience God. In this view of the world, salvation equals a reconciliation that is more thorough than just between God and the individual person.

In many ways, their conversions included a turning away from formalism and professionalism. They encouraged people to leave career paths and secure futures, as if there really was, or is, such a thing. They embraced what I would call *vocational downward mobility*. Success was measured by heavenly means. Francis and Clare embodied spiritual practices that brought these teachings home in their lives. Francis once compared the obedient life of faith to a dead body that does not complain, is immovable, and completely unimpressed by appearances.

Brothers Leo and Angelo and others, sounding like James and John at the Last Supper, once said to Francis, "Tell us the highest form of obedience," and Francis said, "He is most obedient who does not judge why he is moved, does not think about where he is placed, does not ask to be moved, and when he is moved to a higher office, keeps his complete humility by accusing himself all the more while he is being honored."[78]

The Second Order (the Poor Clares) spread almost as rapidly as the First Order had done, and often with the same sort of unpredictability. Just as Francis had done, Clare often sent sisters to other regions and countries without any advance warning to bishops or cardinals ruling those areas. The Poor Clares spread within two decades into France, Spain, Belgium, and Bohemia in these ways. To Spain, for instance, Clare sent

he outlined on brick, he boldly cut the marble and produced the bas-reliefs of his sarcophagi that decorate the museums of Rome and the churches of Ravenna today. In them, we meet again the biblical subjects from the catacombs, but other scenes are added. This richer and more definite symbolism announces that the time of the persecutions was over, and that the holy mysteries no longer needed to be celebrated in secret.

The designers, no longer wanting to express their thoughts in drawing or sculpture alone, turned to speech, as well. The first inscriptions are of a brevity that has its own eloquence. "This is the place of Philemon." Some of them are amplified by means of tender and comforting expressions such as "Florentius, happy little lamb of God." Or, "You have fallen too soon, Constantia, miracle of beauty and wisdom." This was the beginning of a poetry. The spiritual muse no longer could be silent.

—Frederick Ozanam

sisters Agnes (her niece) and Clare (Agnes's niece) by rudderless boat. Like the Irish saints who wandered the seas without sail in order to be led properly by the Holy Spirit, Agnes and Clare shocked the people of Barcelona when they landed on shore and emerged from such a vessel. The women only had to mention who they were and that they were sent from Assisi before they were accepted, and soon the first Poor Clares house was established in Spain.

They were poor, just as Christ was born and died poor. In her *Rule*, Clare wrote: "For the love of the most holy and beloved Child who was wrapped in the poorest swaddling clothes and laid in a manger, and of his most holy Mother, I admonish, beg, and encourage my sisters to always wear only the poorest of garments."[79] She was picking up on something that Francis had instituted for the friars.

Poverty was signaled when Francis chose the cloth for the first Franciscan tunics. The Benedictines wore black, symbolizing humility, and the Cistercians white, for purity. Both choices rested on solid motives, but they also represented the dyeing of cloth into black or white. Francis would have known colors better than anyone in Assisi except for his father, the cloth merchant, whose business it was to search the trade routes for the most alluring dyes and fabrics of the day. Francis would have known that some dyes were made from snails and other animals. But also, Francis saw colors as a form of haughtiness. He is said to have chosen the dirtiest cloth he could find—a sort of dirty brown—for the friars' tunics, but the truth is that he chose a cloth that was a natural color without any preparation necessary.

Cloth without dye may seem trivial, but it had profound symbolism in that day. Many medieval ascetics believed that color itself was a sign of transience and impermanence, and that it may not have existed before the Fall. In the story of Creation, nothing is described in terms of color. Could it be, they wondered, that the devil created the illusion of the first color when he tempted Eve with the forbidden fruit?

When it came to their clothing, Francis and Clare were concerned with poverty in both its appearance (how does it appear to others?) and in its reality (actual money spent). The undyed tunic and cord around the waist presented the first friars with the coarsest, least desirable materials. It was intended to be functional, extremely inexpensive or free, and to appear as a statement of intentional poverty, as well. Such actions only made the first friars appear madder, and less relevant, to those on the outside.

Still, our saints' personalities are never easily grasped, and they were not easygoing people. Just as they rejected color that stood for power or vain beauty, they loved natural color and the species of creation. If some of their contemporaries believed that the devil created the illusion of color in the Garden of Eden, others noticed that God's first act in Creation was light, and without light—as we have known since Isaac Newton—there is no color. So, perhaps all of the colors were created on day one. Francis insisted that the brothers plant flowers so that they might bloom and spin and glorify their Creator, and he reveled in their appearance beside the simple huts at Portiuncula. Clare did the same, and her flower gardens became a special place for Francis to visit.

We can imagine both of them praising the loveliness of *Sister Flowers* along the road or in the garden on one day, marveling at a sunset, appreciating a good song sung well, and complimenting the talented juggler or painter, and then the next day depriving their bodies nearly to starvation, leaving ailments and bodily pain untended to the point of permanent damage. They were probably a constant puzzle to most of their companions and closest friends.

CHAPTER
9

RENEWING THE
BONDS OF CREATION

I n the first fifteen centuries of Christian faith, mystics
and reformers were always at pains to see the universe as
something more than simply rotten. Experiencing God
up close led mystics to see a radical separation of the
spiritual from the material. And the reformers, frustrated at their
inability to change the course and corruption of human events and
mistakes, felt helpless in the face of evil. Francis and Clare were
both mystics and reformers, and they struggled in both of these
directions. Some of their predecessors, such as the leaders of the
Cathar and Albigensian movements, were overcome by them.

The earth was viewed by other mystics as inherently evil,
and all of its creatures, including human beings, hopelessly
fallen. The soul was all that could be saved. For this reason,
the medieval mind saw physical deformities and diseases such
as leprosy as the result of some sort of previous sin. The human
body was seen to be rotting rapidly; saints meditated on skulls
and other symbols of mortality, hoping to focus their minds on
what was heavenly instead.

What sets Francis and Clare apart from the other prophets of
their age—and what, in fact, turns any prophet into a saint—is

their ability to know God intimately as mystics, and to fight for justice as reformers, yet still to view the created universe as good rather than rotten. If it is created, redeemed, and sustained by God the Father, Son, and Holy Spirit, then it is good. Their love for the Creator was one with their love for the creation.

Love was, for them, something more palpable, earthly, and rooted in life than it was for most of their mystic contemporaries. Beatrice of Nazareth (d. 1268), for instance, is typical in speaking of divine love over and against human love. In her treatise *There Are Seven Manners of Loving*, the ultimate rung is a mystic union that removes one completely from earthly existence. There would be altogether different metaphors for this sort of cocoon today, but Beatrice's are unmistakably removed from the creation:

> So the soul has climbed in spirit above time into eternity, it is exalted above all that love can give into the eternity which is love itself, which is beyond time, which is set above all human modes of love, the soul has transcended its own nature in its longing for the life which is there. . . . And now this earth is for the soul a cruel exile and a dire prison and a heavy torment: it despises the world, the earth revolts it, and here is nothing earthly which can console or satisfy it, and it is for the soul a great punishment that it must live in this estrangement and appear so alien.[80]

Francis and Clare were a different sort of mystic. They were more like Buddhism's bodhisattvas who simply will not permit themselves the opportunity to soar into these reaches of enlightenment, but rather set themselves to the task of helping others along their way. We see this again and again in the details of their lives. They exhibited a sensitivity to the living and organic things around them that sets them apart. Francis, for instance, even cared for the inanimate objects of creation with a sensitivity that is similar to Buddhist teachings about kindness toward all sentient beings. In one of his most beautiful paragraphs in *The Golden Legend*, Jacobus of Voragine explains the following about St. Francis:

> The saint would not handle lanterns and candles because he did not want to dim their brightness with his hands. He walked reverently on stones out of respect for him who was called Peter, which means stone. He lifted worms from the road for fear they might be trampled underfoot by passersby. Bees might perish in the cold of winter, so he had honey and fine wines set out for them. He called all animals brothers and sisters. When he looked at the sun, the moon, and the stars, he was filled with inexpressible joy by his love of the Creator and invited them all to love their Creator.[81]

The earthiness of early Franciscan love was rooted in the earth itself. Francis and Clare shared a pre-Copernican view of the universe (Nicolaus Copernicus, d. 1543). The pre-Copernican view imagined earth at the center of the universe and humankind at the center of everything. This perspective permeates much of Christian tradition, including the Psalms and the translators of the King James Bible. But you wouldn't know that Francis and Clare looked at the created world with this lens by reading their writings or the stories of their lives. They brought new life to the psalms that were loved and prayed by Jesus himself, such as this passage from Psalm 8: "When I consider thy heavens, the work of thy fingers / the moon and the stars, which thou hast ordained; / What is man, that thou art mindful of him? / and the son of man, that thou visitest him?" (KJV). But they also showed how it is possible to look up at the skies and all around at the creatures of creation, praising and blessing God as a Creator who nevertheless does not value only humans.[82] The human being shares the universe with other created beings in the early Franciscan worldview.

We rarely see either Francis or Clare doing typical religious things in traditional religious places. Valleys and hilltops became Francis's field of faith. He found God in the woods and in creatures as often as he did in churches. Sacred and profane were designations of geography and location before their lives and teachings brought them much closer together.

By the official teachings of the day, an altar was supposed to be present in order for prayer and sacraments to take place. The late Middle Ages was the era of only religion, not spirituality. Local bishops would sanction a new religious space by blessing the altar inside a church or chapel. The laity—other than the very rich—did not own personal prayer books. Even private devotions were said in church, usually before or after Mass or Matins. For many people, singing or saying the Latin liturgical hours or Paternosters ("Our Fathers") was possible only when led by the clergy or a monastic community. A sacred place in and of itself, a church was the primary space for experiencing God. Many medieval chronicles detail how pilgrims would sometimes travel to a church only to find its doors closed. Rather than go elsewhere, they would pray while kneeling outside or while touching the outside wall with a hand or head.

Early Franciscanism brought changes to all of this. By preaching to the people in piazzas and other public places, Francis signaled that God's Word was active outside of church. There was a sense in which the words of prayer, piety, and preaching were seen to partake sacramentally of the Word Itself, and creativity entered into one's experience of God. In song and poetry sung in the vernacular, they made spirituality seem possible to those who were untrained in formal religion. Spirituality at home began to be possible. The distinctions between a theologically literate clergy class and an obedient, pious laity class began to break down. Franciscans led the way, through the creation of what was called the "Third Order" of Franciscans (in 1221), in finding ways for laypeople to live vowed lives of spiritual significance, but without leaving behind the world of family, jobs, or other responsibilities. It was also at this time that letter writing became an important vehicle for spiritual encouragement, personal Bible reading and study grew, and discussions of theological issues in the workplace originated.

In the decades and centuries immediately after Francis and Clare, home altars became common in Italy. These were places set aside in the home, still common in some Catholic homes today, where a person would replicate the setting of a church for purposes of personal prayer, adding images, icons, rosary beads, and mementos of various kinds. Before Francis and Clare, we have little evidence of these. Similarly, vernacular spiritual writing was almost nonexistent before Francis and Clare. But in the century after their deaths, the lives of Francis penned by Thomas of Celano were among the most popular choices for daily reading, and the vernacular Italian works of spirituality became almost too many to count.[83]

CARING FOR CREATURES

The connection between Francis of Assisi and animals is the single fact about him that most people know. We have tales of his encounters with animals, fish, invertebrates, and plants. In all of these ways, Franciscans emphasized that creation includes more than humankind. Just as they redefined what it means to be family, they further widened the fraternity to link humans and creatures in the same relationship with God.

On one warm afternoon, Francis wandered outside of Assisi, questioning his motives for ministry, asking God if perhaps everything he had done up until that point had been for the wrong reasons. He wondered if he should have simply gotten married and raised a family as his father wanted him to do. Francis was always the most critical of himself, but it was on just such an afternoon that Francis first met the birds and spoke to them as if to equals. That day marks the beginning of the environmental movement, the beginning of the era when we began to understand ourselves as intrinsically connected to all of creation.

Many other legends arose surrounding Francis's love for animals, and chief among them were stories about the Wolf of Gubbio—whom Francis tamed of his savagery in exchange for a commitment from the townspeople of Gubbio to feed him for the rest of his life. In the early twentieth century, a book called *The Chronicles of Brother Wolf* brought the wolf to life again as a full-fledged disciple of Francis. These newer legends were written in the spirit of those friars who regretted the institutional turn taken by the Order after Francis's death.

In "Brother Wolf Joins the Poor Clares," the anonymous author tells of how the friars in charge disdained the wolf after Francis's death, and how the wolf eventually went to live with the sisters instead. "Now among some of the Brothers was a certain dislike of Brother Wolf, which after our master's death showed itself in various words and murmurings, scorning and spurning and pushing aside. No food was put out for him, and no water, which was worse, and Tertius [the friar-narrator of these tales] fared little better, so that there was nothing to share with Brother Wolf."

After this rude treatment of Francis's brother Wolf, the creature is driven away with a stick by one of the friars. He wanders briefly, imagining that he might return to Gubbio, but instead finds his way to San Damiano, where he waits outside for a short time with an injured foot.

> When they opened the door wide [Brother Wolf] crept inside, looking upon them with eyes that were full of tears and pain. And they too, when they saw the evil case that he was in, and that foot, fell to mourning as women will, and very quickly they summoned the Sisters, though it was past Compline, when none may speak, but they with warm water and soft oils washed and dressed it and bound it up. . . . After that he lived with [the Poor Clares] and left them no more.[84]

This may indicate that dedication to caring for creatures as equals with humans fell off after the deaths of Francis and Clare.

The stories of Francis are also full of birds of a variety of species, including falcons, doves, pheasants, crows, and others. On one occasion, a small waterbird landed on the side of the boat he was traveling in on his way to Greccio. The bird nested in Francis's hands, like a cat might do in one's lap, and Francis blessed it. Later, when Francis arrived at the Greccio hermitage, a falcon "covenanted with him" and undertook to make noise each evening at the hour when Francis would rise to say the liturgy of the hours. The falcon would do the same in the early morning as well, except on those occasions when Francis was ill, when he would remain silent. On another occasion, we hear of a rich man in Siena who sent a pheasant to Francis when the saint was known to be ill. The pheasant was supposed to be killed in order to provide much-needed meat that would strengthen the constitution of all who ate it. Meat was often prescribed in those days as a remedy for curing illness. But Francis, of course, did not slaughter the bird but rejoiced over it and spoke with it. The pheasant lived for a time with the friars and took to hiding under their tunics in their cells when the friars attempted to remove the bird to the outdoors.[85]

CRICKETS, FISH, LAMBS, AND BEES

Just as he had encouraged the birds to sing, Francis did the same with a cricket at Portiuncula. "Sing, Sister Cricket," he instructed the creature, which was sitting in the bushes beside his cell. He held out his hand and the cricket sat upon it and sang. This happened again and again for eight days. The same thing happened when a fisherman on the lake in Rieti caught a fish and presented it to Francis. Rather than keep the fish for food, Francis set it back into the water. The fish followed the boat for some time afterwards and would depart only when Francis blessed it.

We have numerous stories of Francis with lambs. Lambs have, since the days of the ancient Israelites, been associated with God's redemption. The cousin of Christ, John the Baptist, mysteriously announced to his audience as Jesus approached, "Look, there is the Lamb of God who takes away the sin of the world." And St. Paul later cleared this up, by referring to Jesus as "the Passover lamb," a gloss on the Jewish Scriptures that forever linked Christ with the freedom of slaves that happened long before in Egypt. Jesus himself told the parable of the lost sheep, and that lost animal was a lamb in the eyes of Francis:

> So he told them this parable: "Which one of you with a hundred sheep, if he lost one, would fail to leave the ninety-nine in the desert and go after the missing one till he found it? And when he found it, would he not joyfully take it on his shoulders and then, when he got home, call together his friends and neighbours, saying to them, 'Rejoice with me, I have found my sheep that was lost.' In the same way, I tell you, there will be more rejoicing in heaven over one sinner repenting than over ninety-nine upright people who have no need of repentance."[86]

Bonaventure's *Life* of Francis explains that the saint loved lambs because "he had a special tenderness for the creatures that by their likeness and nature demonstrate the gentleness of Christ, and because they are a type for Him who was already known in the Old Testament."[87]

Just as he did with turtledoves and other creatures, Francis would barter or raise money to buy back lambs, saving them from slaughter. Symbolism meant nothing to him; he would care for lambs as Jesus had done, because he looked on these gentle creatures as if they were Christ himself. He once mourned the death of a lamb, "in the presence of all," according to Bonaventure, that had been killed by another animal. Lambs became Francis's most earnest animal audiences. For anyone who has tried speaking to animals of various kinds, it is much easier to imagine a congregation of lambs listening to Francis speak, anxious but steady eyes fixed on his every movement, than it is to imagine birds paying attention. The tales of Francis and lambs are almost too many to count. The creatures showed various acts of piety, such as bowing a knee at the altar to the Virgin in Portiuncula, and are often spoken of as the pupils of the Poverello.

Francis always called creatures his brothers and sisters, but most often, he called them sisters. There is a strong sense of the mother in Francis's metaphors and in his spiritual guidance. At one point, Francis compares himself to a hen caring for her chicks. He also encourages the brothers to be mothers to one another. He clung to the feminine side of God, cherishing those metaphors that not only broaden our understanding of who God is, but also temper the over-emphasis that has always existed on the masculine in God. Francis adored God as Mother and he and Clare both sought to imitate Christ, but also the Virgin Mary, the mother of God. It is only by discovering the mothering, loving, caring nature of God in Christ that the world will be healed of its pain and sorrow, Francis believed. As one scholar has put it, "The authoritarian father of Francis wasn't a possible Christian model of a good ruler. Therefore Francis chooses to be a mother."[88]

Justice   *Injustice*

We even have stories of creatures that have come to rest and play in places where Francis once was. Bees—which have long been symbols of sanctity for their hardworking ability to create sweetness without taking away from any other creature—took up residence in the ceramic cup that he used for drinking while on Mt. Alverno. Sometime after he had left the mountain, the cup was seen there, full of honeycomb. There is a sense that the presence and touch of Francis improved the expansion of God's creative activity.

In some tales, we may reasonably doubt when the author tells us that fish and crickets left Francis's presence only when the saint

gave them permission to do so. Francis was surely not a program-
mer of animal and insect minds and actions. But there is no need
to doubt that Francis had an ability to touch creatures in a way
that is unavailable to most of us.[89] He learned a sort of sensitivity
to the earth and its creatures that eludes most people.

There are very few similar stories of Clare engaged with
creatures. Her life was lived primarily indoors, and her experiences were not so much with animals as they were with
people. She was a healer of human sickness and a counselor of
troubled souls. One gets the sense that Francis enjoyed caring
for creatures himself, but often brought troubled people to
Clare. In fact, when we do encounter Clare with a creature
in one of the early texts, it almost seems to be portrayed by
the editors as a *sanctifying* of the Francis tradition, taking it
further away from reality, and so further away from what is
believable.

The primary example of this can be found in the story of
Clare and a fierce wolf that was plaguing the people of Assisi.
This tale is told in *The Versified Legend of the Virgin Clare*, a
document compiled immediately after the canonization process
had ended.[90] Clearly in the tradition of Francis and the Wolf
of Gubbio, we see Clare also facing the terrors of a wolf that is
hurting people, even eating them. Francis had brokered peace,
emphasizing the ways in which animal and human creation are
intertwined, and had respected the beast as well as the people.
But in Clare's story with the wolf, she never actually enters the
woods, encounters the animal, or discusses a solution with anyone.
According to the tale, a mother of twin boys has already lost one
of them to the jaws of a wolf when another wolf breaks into her
home and steals away the other boy. The wolf drags the child into

the forest and the mother cries aloud to Clare (probably in prayer, rather than in person, although the setting is unclear), begging her for help. The neighbors search for the boy, and eventually find him; the wolf has left deep bite marks on the boy's neck and body, but he has ultimately left the child, presumably after the prayer was offered to Clare.

> His mother runs to Clare herself,
> shows her son's scars to everyone,
> and offers her praises to God and to Clare.

The immediacy and earthy relevance of the Franciscan spirit are already being lost in the transmission of the tradition, and in this sanctifying of it. Clare's work is interpreted as of the more divine, wonder-working sort. We see the same sort of change in the stories of St. Anthony of Padua, who was one of the most prominent Franciscans in the years immediately following Francis's death. Like Francis, Anthony preached, but in Anthony's case it was to fish, not birds, and he did not preach to them out of love but in order to demonstrate to a crowd of heretics in Rimini that they should believe without reason (as fish would do). The story in *The Little Flowers* is lengthy, and features the fish coming partially out of the water to nod their heads "in peace and gentleness" as the saint talked. Later, the same fish have listened to Anthony's words and they not only stick their heads out of the water but they "open their mouths . . . to give praise to God."

These experiences of Clare and Anthony lack the earthy understanding that Francis seemed to possess. On the Feast of the Nativity, for instance, he would insist that oxen and donkeys be "spoiled with extra feed and softer hay" because they had kept the Christ child warm on that first day.[91] He practiced a close relationship with creatures that was as uncommon then as it is now. Like no saint before him, Francis desired to touch the earth and also be touched by it.

10

BEING CRUCIFIED
WITH CHRIST

In the legends of Francis of Assisi there is no greater pinnacle of spiritual imitation than in his encounter with Christ in the form of a six-winged angel. This happened while he was meditating alone on Mt. Alverno in the Apennine mountains of central Italy. It was September 1224, probably sometime between the Feast of the Exaltation of the Holy Cross (the 14th) and the Feast of St. Michael the Archangel (the 29th), as two of the early texts mention each and its proximity to the event. Francis's closest companions were nearby. They had arrived at the mountain about one month earlier to have a Lenten experience, according to Francis, despite the fact that it would have been closer to Advent than to Lent at that time of year. The Feast of the Assumption, on August 15, is probably when they began their stay on Alverno, and Francis intended to stay and pray for forty days (a *Lent*), until the Feast of St. Michael.

As their stay went on, Francis gradually desired to be more and more alone. A bridge separated Francis's little hut from those of his brothers, and the texts tell us that on one occasion, when Francis did not answer his call, Brother Leo came to see that he was all right. There, Leo saw Francis kneeling in the woods in a mystical ecstasy. Leo later recalled having seen a flaming torch above the saint's head, and a bright light. On one of the following days, the same sort of experience happened to Francis again, but this time while he was completely alone. No friars or friends saw what happened. Francis later told a select few of them that he had had a vision of a six-winged angel, known as a seraph, looking down at him.

The seraph was a symbol of profound holiness and purification that Christians know from the Hebrew prophet Isaiah:

In the year that King Uzziah died, I saw the Lord sitting on a throne, high and lofty; and the hem of his robe filled the temple. Seraphs were in attendance above him; each had six wings: with two they covered their faces, and with two they covered their feet, and with two they flew. And one called to another and said:

"Holy, holy, holy is the Lord of hosts;
the whole earth is full of his glory."

The pivots on the thresholds shook at the voices of those who called, and the house filled with smoke. And I said: "Woe is me! I am lost, for I am a man of unclean lips, and I live among a people of unclean lips; yet my eyes have seen the King, the Lord of hosts!"

Then one of the seraphs flew to me, holding a live coal that had been taken from the altar with a pair of tongs.[92]

This wasn't the first occasion that an image of Christ had communicated with Francis; the encounter with the crucifix of San

Damiano had happened some fifteen or sixteen years earlier. But in contrast to the crucifix, the seraph on the mountainside did not speak; there was no voice of God this time. Overwhelming light is part of the description that dominates all of the early narratives of what happened, all of which must surely stem from Brother Leo, the only friar close to Francis during that retreat on Alverno.

As we have noted, Francis was nearly blind by this time in his life. His eyes were crying all the time and his vision was seriously impaired. Only in the last one hundred years have scholars begun to suggest scientific reasons for why Francis cried so often in his last decade. Alban Butler (of the old-school hagiographers) wrote about 250 years ago, echoing a tale from *The Little Flowers*: "He was endowed with an extraordinary gift of tears. His eyes seemed two fountains of tears, which were almost continually falling from them, insomuch that at length he almost lost his sight." Butler goes on to explain that Francis's physicians implored him to cry less, because it was the tears that were deepening his eye problem and pain. It is as if Francis's holiness caused his physical suffering to deepen. We know today that the opposite was most likely true. We can now suppose that Francis suffered from an eye disease such as glaucoma. Medieval physicians often confused symptoms with maladies. Their age was one that spiritualized physical realities, making them into spiritual evidences.

For Francis to see anything with clarity at this time would have itself been a miracle. The six-winged seraph was not a product of his imagination—I am not suggesting that—but if sense perceptions are determined by the abilities of our senses in addition to our beliefs about what we think we have seen, then the seraph that Francis saw is not the seraph that Leo would have seen, had Leo seen it!

William of Auvergne and Robert Grosseteste, two contemporaries of Francis, were teaching theories of perception at the University of Paris at the precise time that Francis was on the mountain.[93] Both William and Robert studied light from philosophical and mathematical perspectives. They immersed themselves in Plato's, Aristotle's, and Galen's writings on these subjects, articulating what they called a metaphysics of light. Roger Bacon did the same, following in their footsteps thirty years later, and then, after teaching for twenty years in Paris, became a Franciscan in 1256. Are thoughts dependent on sight? How does the human eye *grasp* what it sees? In Genesis 1:3 when God created the first light (before sun and moon), how did that act relate to Christ the Light of the World (John 1)? These were the sorts of questions that occupied scholars during Francis's day.

Scholarship was wedded to religious instruction and understanding in the early centuries of university life. Both William of Auvergne and Robert Grosseteste, in fact, later became bishops. All their work was aimed at explaining how God works in and through natural phenomena. Robert Grosseteste even offers an explanation that would rationalize, or perhaps just spiritualize, visions such as the one that resulted in Francis's stigmata, the implanting of the wounds of Christ on his flesh:

> I therefore say that there is a spiritual light that floods over intelligible objects and over the mind's eye—that is related to the interior eye and to intelligible objects just as the corporeal sun relates to the bodily eye and to corporeal visible objects.[94]

All of this was of no interest to people like Francis and Clare. Theirs was a simplicity of mind that follows from a certain kind of obedience that comes from an experience of presence. When mystics feel that God is with them, or within them, why would speculation still be necessary? Questions of perception never dogged Francis, even when children were throwing mud at him in the streets of Assisi.

The seraph itself exhibited the five wounds. *The Legend of the Three Companions* explains that "within its wings was the form of a beautiful, crucified man, with hands and feet extended as if on a cross, and whose features were just as those of Jesus Christ."[95] Both Bonaventure and *The Little Flowers* add detail to compare the wings of the seraph with the wings of the seraph from the passage in Isaiah quoted above, saying, "Two of the wings were raised above his head, two were spread out in flight, and the other two covered the whole body." Francis stood there and adored the seraph. He marveled at it, and also sorrowed for Christ crucified, who was looking down upon him. *The Little Flowers* says beautifully that "Francis was so afraid, but yet filled with sweetness and sorrow mingled with wonder." This must have gone on for quite some time, as Francis gazed at the seraph and the Crucified One gazed back at him.

Somehow at that moment, Christ, in the form of that seraph, transmitted the wounds of stigmata to Francis. There was a brilliant light similar to the one that Leo had overseen on the earlier occasion. Two years later, after Francis died and the announcement was made to the world about his stigmata, there were numerous stories in Umbria about that light, of people saying that they had seen it, too.

St. Francis Receiving the Stigmata

The stigmata wounds were seared into his flesh—one in each palm, one in each foot, and a piercing in his right side. They were painful and bloody—both of which phenomena Francis tried desperately to cover up for the last two years of his life. The wound in Francis's side always appeared "unhealed, enflamed, and bleeding," according to *The Little Flowers*. The early chroniclers tell us of friars and cardinals and others trying to sneak glimpses of them, and Francis wearing shoes, extra garments, and so on, to conceal them.

Francis did not tell a soul at first, although eventually he did. Bonaventure says, "Eventually, he understood from this . . . ," and *The Little Flowers* similarly says, "Later, he marveled at what an amazing and undeserved vision he had had." Most likely, the friars came to know about the wounds by accident, when they had to wash Francis's clothes. It is probably then that the courageous ones—those who knew him best—asked, and were told. At some point, Leo was allowed to help Francis care for the wounds with washing and dressings.

Francis's stigmata wounds were the first recorded instance of this miracle in history. It is easy to forget that fact these days, when the miracle has been reasonably claimed dozens of times over the last several centuries. Most recently and prominently, the Capuchin friar St. Padre Pio is said to have experienced the wounds in the middle of the twentieth century and, since he lived in the age of television and photography, we have hundreds of photographs showing Padre Pio wearing bloody coverings for the wounds in his hands so as to hide the sanctity as best he could.[96] Francis also covered up his wounds, and only those closest to him came to know of them prior to his death.

LETTING THE WORLD KNOW

Scholars believe that it was most likely within days (or perhaps, the very evening) of Francis's death that Elias, the minister-general of the Order, wrote his letter announcing the death of Francis, mentioning for the first time the wounds of Christ found on his body. Elias was in the immediate stages of grief when he wrote his letter. He begins by writing, "Before I begin to speak, I sigh," and "my groans gush forth," speaking of fears and dreads being fulfilled in the events that have just happened. He acknowledges the immense loss to the world and to the Order and also to himself, saying, "he has left me in the midst of darkness." But after the sadness is past (Elias warns everyone not to mourn for long), he explains that a miracle has happened: "Not long before his death, our brother and father appeared crucified, bearing in his body the five wounds which are truly the marks of Christ."[97] Elias's notice sounds almost startled, as if he has just been brought into the circle of those who knew this miracle two years earlier. He records that the wounds were known to emit blood, a sign that he had spoken to those who were closest to Francis and had seen the same, firsthand. This is the first recorded word of what had happened.

In 1262, more than thirty-five years after Francis's death, Friar Jordan of Giano, best known for his work on behalf of the Order in Germany, recounted: "After the death of Blessed Francis, Brother Elias, who was his vicar, addressed a letter of consolation to the brothers throughout the Order who were dismayed over the death of so great a father. He announced to one and all, as Blessed Francis had commanded him, that he blessed them all on his behalf and absolved them from every fault. Furthermore, he made known to them the stigmata and the other miracles which the Most High God had deigned to perform through Blessed Francis after his death."[98] However, one of the early texts also tells us of some other people, perhaps including friars, who doubted the stigmata and its authenticity. *The Legend of the Three Companions*, written about the same time as Thomas of Celano's *Second Life* of Francis, mentions "many people who looked unkindly on the man of God and doubted the stigmata," leaving us without details, intrigued to know more.[99] We also have evidence that Pope Gregory IX did not accept calling the wounds stigmata at the time of canonizing Francis. It took Gregory IX ten years, in fact, to call them that.[100]

PRECEDENTS AND MEANINGS

Thomas of Celano sounds downright philosophical in his *Second Life* when he summarizes: "Perhaps the cross of our Lord had to appear in the flesh [to Francis], since it could never be explained in words. Therefore, let silence speak where words are empty."[101] But we should try to say a little something more.

Francis was not the first person to embrace Christ on the cross in a way that achieved some sort of identity or unity with his object. Christian tradition is replete with examples of men and women practicing a devotion to the crucifix that results in some sort of physical identification with the Crucified. St. Paul said in Galatians, chapter two: "I have been crucified with Christ; and it is no longer I who live, but it is Christ who lives in me. And the life I now live in the flesh I live by faith in the Son of God, who loved me and gave himself for me." Francis would also have known the story of St. Bernard of Clairvaux, who was once praying alone in church, lying prostrate on the floor, when Christ separated his arms from the crossbar of the cross in order to embrace him. I once saw a statue of St. Ludmilla, as well (it was for sale on eBay), showing Christ unfixing himself from the cross in order to embrace her.

Many a mystic has stood or kneeled before the Crucified Christ, adoring him and imagining embracing him. And then, after Francis's experience, there were many others to come.

After Clare's death, Bonaventure wrote a letter to a Poor Clare sister, saying:

> Draw near . . . with loving feet to Jesus wounded, to Jesus crowned with thorns, to Jesus fastened to the gibbet of the cross; and be not content, as the blessed apostle Thomas was, merely to see in his hands the print of the nails or to thrust your hand into his side; but rather go right in, through the opening in his side, to the very heart of Jesus where, transformed by most burning love for Christ, held by the nails of divine love, pierced by the lance of profound charity . . . you will know no other wish or desire.[102]

It is difficult to tell if this sort of language was a spiritualizing of the meaning of stigmata, or advice on the right approach to replicating it. Salimbene even wrote in the 1280s of a disturbed friar who was led by a voice to partially crucify himself in order to fully identify himself with Christ. They found him fastened by nails, all but one hand.

There are many ways to embrace Christ. Thomas of Celano describes Clare as "drunk on her tears for the Passion of Christ." Particularly during the offices of prayer that were said each afternoon, Thomas says, she felt penitence most deeply, "wishing to sacrifice her life for the One who was sacrificed."[103] In the centuries before Francis and Clare, mystics often meditated on the crucifix; they focused on the eyes of Jesus, the arms held open, the kiss of his mouth, comparing it to Song of Songs 1:2, "Let him kiss me with the kisses of his mouth!" and feeling the wound in his side.

Gazing meditation was common for medieval mystics. Very little of this survives today. A century ago, the Irish poet W. B.

Yeats offered this simple "Drinking Song" that communicates something rather profound: "Wine comes in at the mouth / And love comes in at the eye; / That's all we shall know for truth / Before we grow old and die." When Francis and Clare gazed at an object, they absorbed it in ways unrealized even among religious people today; love came in at the eye. We barely pause long enough to consider ourselves, let alone to consider objects outside of our bodies. We will look at a sunset or some other piece of scenery, but we rarely gaze with what might be called the eyes of the soul, as saints once did.

The medieval imagination was geared toward the visual. Seeing the consecrated host of the Eucharist, for example, was a profoundly moving experience for many. It was uncommon to see it in those days, and still less common to receive it; and it was to the medieval imagination the crucified body of Christ made miraculously present. To see the Eucharist was to be transformed in some small way by it. There were cults or followings of the Eucharist just as there were cults of popular saints. Looking simply or disinterestedly at icons was uncommon, while gazing at them and looking into their eyes was quite common. The ancient tradition of covering images in church on solemn occasions, such as Good Friday, stems from the idea that all eyes should be down at these times—including the eyes of the images looking back at us.

When Francis looked at a crucifix, or when Clare looked on a sick man or woman left in her care, they each beheld a reality that is much deeper and more inscrutable than sight alone may determine. Their will was as creative as their vision, both of which combined to see reality in symbols and the stuff before their eyes as the raw material of God. Francis and Clare gazed, not just looked, and they perceived as much as they saw. By today's standards, these qualities make them unusual, the sort of people that most of us wouldn't ever invite for dinner. However, we might remember the instruction of Thomas à Kempis: "There is an incomparable distance between the things people imagine by reason, and those that illuminated people behold by contemplation."

The six-winged seraph in the form of the crucified Christ is rarely understood as the love symbol that it was for Francis and his contemporaries. When the troubadour poets had dramatically praised their lovesickness as "the wounds of love," they were secularizing (and trivializing) an ancient Christian way of describing Christ as both a lover and a seeker of lovers. The Lord who loves us on the cross is also the One who pursues us, and even pierces our hearts with love's arrows. One historian has summarized this tradition as "Christ as Cupid."[104]

The Old Testament Song of Songs showed first to Jews and then Christians that God has always loved with an intensity that *wounds*: "You have ravished my heart, my sister, my bride, you have ravished my heart with a glance of your eyes, with one jewel of your necklace" (4:9). Ideas and images such as the pierced heart, the flaming heart, and the Sacred Heart of Jesus all had their origins in these same traditions. In the fifth century, St. Augustine of Hippo wrote in book nine of his *Confessions*: "Thou hadst pierced our hearts with Thy charity, and we carried Thy words as it were fixed in our entrails."[105] In her autobiography, written more than a millennium later, St. Teresa of Avila describes a mystical encounter with an angel, using words almost verbatim from Augustine:

In his hands I saw a long golden spear and at the end of the iron tip I seemed to see a point of fire. With this he seemed to pierce my heart several times so that it penetrated to my entrails. When he drew it out, I thought he was drawing them out with it and he left me completely afire with a great love for God.[106]

The most passionate love between God and human is bitter-sweet. A mystic will tell you that is why not everyone wants to love God. In the century before Francis and Clare, the Cistercian Gilbert of Hoyland meditated on the passion of Christ, wishing for himself what later happened to Francis: "Would that [Christ] might multiply such wounds in me, from the sole of my foot to the crown of my head, that there might be no health in me! For health is evil without the wounds that Christ's gracious gaze inflicts."[107] That is just what occurred on the quiet mountainside when Francis met the seraph, alone.

For two years, Francis kept this incredible secret from all but those closest to him. All that was left for him was to keep pleading with the brothers to follow the original intentions of the *Rule*. In his final writing, the *Testament*, Francis pledged his eternal obedience to the ministers-general of the Order, but also said to all future ministers-general that they were bound by obedience (to Francis, perhaps, and to God) "not to add to or take away from" those original ideals in the *Rule*, reiterated in the *Testament*. As he lay dying, he asked his brothers to sing his beloved *Canticle of the Creatures* in Italian, rather than the usual prayers and songs in ecclesiastical Latin. They probably also sang the Ave Maria, in honor of the Virgin Mary, to whom Francis was always dearly devoted.

Hail Mary, full of grace,
the Lord is with you.
Blessed are you among women,
and blessed is the fruit of your womb, Jesus.
Holy Mary, Mother of God,
pray for us sinners
now and at the hour of our death.
Amen.

He died late on Saturday, October 4, 1226. The friars carried the body from Portiuncula, where he breathed his last, back into Assisi on Sunday morning. Bonaventure says that people from all around joined them in procession carrying tree branches and flaming candles. They began the journey early in the morning at the break of dawn, as the birds were rousing the city.

THE CANTICLE OF THE CREATURES

All of the sources tell us that Francis insisted on feeling the earth on his body just before his death. The medieval assumption was that every Christian should want to die in a holy place—in other words, in a church—if possible. If salvation was possible only in the Church, then the church was the place that all wished to be at the moment of passing. A good life made possible a good and appropriate death, which would include solemn Masses, general confession, and last rites from the hands of a priest. In these ways, the Church was brought to the dying, even if the dying couldn't make it to church.

Remarkably, there is no mention in the poignant fourteen chapters of Bonaventure's *Life* of Francis of Masses, confessions, and last rites. As Francis was dying, he wanted to be taken back to St. Mary of the Angels—Portiuncula. But on the way there he asked to be laid on the bare ground. *The Little Flowers* has Francis saying to the brothers who were carrying him, "Lay me down on the ground. Turn me to face Assisi." Bonaventure added with feeling that Francis laid himself on the ground naked, which usually meant without habit or cowl, but still some sort of undergarment. "He prostrated himself with passion and spirit, naked on the bare earth." And Thomas of Celano in his *Second Life* shows Francis doing the same, looking to heaven, and then saying to the friars who were gathered there, "Now, I have done what is mine to do. May Christ teach you what is yours to do!"

LOVE FOR LIFE AND DEATH

Just as human and animal combined in the worldview of Francis and Clare, so too, life and death were intertwined. "In the midst of life we are in death," says the ancient funeral rite. No era knew this fact as well as the Middle Ages.

When Francis was nearly blind a year before his death, he composed that remarkable hymn *The Canticle of the Creatures.* In the song, he expresses his belief that the wildness and expectancies of nature are part of God's plan for human life. This marked the true dividing point—the first real signpost—for what has become the modern understanding of how earth and heaven join together. As one contemporary author has put it:

> The *Canticle* signifies that the whole creation is a cosmic Incarnation—earth, air, water, sun, moon, stars—all are related to Brother Sun who is the splendor and radiance of the Most High. We might read Francis' *Canticle* as foreshadowing the new creation, when we will find ourselves related to all things in the spirit of reconciliation and peace.[108]

It all began with Francis of Assisi's fear of mice. Two years before his death, Francis was living in a small hut outside the walls of San Damiano in a place that Clare had prepared for him among the gardens. His eyesight was getting so poor at this time that he suffered constant pain from both sunlight and from simply opening his eyes. He was growing blinder by the day. After only sixty days at San Damiano, he was unable to see at all.

The description in the text[109] says that what happened next was a temptation of the devil. It was "by divine permission that for increase of his affliction and his merit"—mice began to infest his hut. "So many mice came into his cell that they were running all over his body and all around him both night and day. They kept him from resting as well as from praying. Even when he tried to eat, the mice swarmed onto his table and infested him by the multitude." It is difficult to read such a description without checking around one's feet!

Francis responded by praying to God: "Look on me and comfort me in my afflictions, so that I may endure them with patience!" He had reason to be upset; first blindness, then an infestation!

Jesus responded to him "in spirit," in other words, through non-verbal communication that is heard in the soul: "If a certain man was given a treasure so great and precious that the whole earth was as nothing compared to it, wouldn't he rejoice despite any infirmities or afflictions he might experience? Be glad, brother, and rejoice in your difficulties. As for the rest, take heed of them no more than you would if you had already entered My kingdom!"

Francis rose the next morning and began to compose his *Canticle*. He began by integrating the natural and the spiritual in a way that deliberately honored those creatures and aspects of Creation that we normally either forget or despise. He said to his brother friars: "I must add to the praise of God, our own consolation, and the edification of our neighbor, a new song of praise for those creatures of God that we use every day and without whom we are unable to live. If we do not praise them, we must terribly offend their Creator. For continually we show ourselves ungrateful for so great grace and so many blessings, not praising the Lord and giver of all."

Most high, almighty, good Lord God,
    to you belong all praise, glory, honor, and blessing!
Praised be you, O my Lord and God, with all your creatures,
    and especially our Brother Sun,
    who brings us the day and who brings us the light.
He is fair and shines with a very great splendor:
    O Lord, he signifies you to us!
Praised be you, O my Lord, for our Brother Wind,
    and for air and cloud, calms and all weather
    through which you uphold life in all creatures.
Praise the Lord for our Sister Water,
    who is very useful to us and humble
    and precious and clean.
Praise the Lord for our Brother Fire,
    through whom you give us light in the darkness.
He is bright and pleasant and very mighty and strong.
Praise the Lord for our Mother Earth,
    who sustains us and keeps us,
    and brings forth the grass and all
    of the fruits and flowers of many colors.

Once the *Canticle* was composed and Francis had taught his companions to sing it, he then saw need to add another verse. The bishop of Assisi was then arguing with the local governor so fiercely that the bishop excommunicated the governor and the governor forbade any citizen to enter into any contract with the bishop. The text[110] tells us that Francis was grieved when he heard of their bickering, but "most of all he was grieved that no one had gotten between them to try and make peace." And so, Francis wrote this verse for his song, which speaks to the need for mediating justice and peace between the powers of the world.

> Praise be you, O my Lord, for all who show forgiveness and
> > pardon one another for your sake,
> > and who endure weakness and tribulation.
> Blessed are they who peaceably endure,
> For you, Most High, shall give them a crown.

He told one of his companions to ask the governor to come to the bishop's house along with the officials of the city. Francis was too sick to go, but he sent instructions with his companions, probably Leo, Angelo, and Rufinus, that they were to sing the *Canticle* before the gathering and "have trust in the Lord that he will humble their hearts." This is how it happened: the governor was the first to apologize, asking for the bishop's forgiveness, and the bishop accepted and embraced him once again as a brother.

And last, Francis made room for death in his great song.[111] He could hardly open his eyes, and any sunlight was painful to him. "Brother Ass," he had once called his own body, comparing it to the beast of burden that never does all that its master requires of it. But Francis transformed his discomfort into praise for those parts of earthly existence that most challenged him. Once he was told by his doctors and companions that his infirmities were beyond healing, the time had come to look forward to death, and he did.

He asked for Leo and Angelo to come to his side and sing to him of Sister Death. Francis had written the last verse:

Praise to you, O my Lord, for our Sister Death
and the death of the body from whom no one may escape.
Woe to those who die in mortal sin.
but blessed are they who are found walking by your most holy
    will,
For the second death
    shall have no power to do them any harm.
Praise to you, O my Lord, and all blessing.
We give you thanks and serve you with great humility.

This vernacular song has been sung ever since, by Franciscans and others. The attention paid by Francis to the creatures has led many scholars to draw fascinating connections between his emphasis on looking with fresh eyes on the created world with the renaissance of interest in geometry and the study of light and visual perspective that followed. The Byzantine era of painting was dark, featuring idealized figures, but what emerged from the Italian painters Cimabue and Giotto in the thirteenth and fourteenth centuries was a renewed attention to real life, details of the human figure and all manner of creatures, and a perspective of light that hadn't been seen since the classical era. Many of those famous paintings are reproduced in black and white throughout this book. The generation that was Francis's and Clare's represented the one before Scholasticism was born in Paris; before Bonaventure and Thomas Aquinas (both d. 1274) lovingly combined a scholar's mind with a mystic's heart; before architecture soared with new expression for God's splendor in Gothic forms; and before Cimabue (d. ca. 1302) and Giotto (d. 1337) brought realism and light back to painting.

Detail of "Pilate and the Priests"

THE SEPULCHER OF ST. FRANCIS

I n the last years before his death, Francis visited Clare and the sisters at San Damiano after being pestered to do so by the friars and by Clare, and he responded with one of his most dramatic gestures. Instead of preaching as he was expected to do, Francis sat down before the gathering and had ashes poured all around him in a circle. Then he took an additional container of ashes and poured them over his head. After a short time, he stood and began to recite Psalm 51, his favorite prayer of confession. It goes, in part, like this:

> Have mercy on me, O God, according to your loving-kindness; in your great compassion blot out my offenses.
>
> Wash me through and through from my wickedness and cleanse me from my sin.
>
> …
>
> Create in me a clean heart, O God, and renew a right spirit within me.
>
> Cast me not away from your presence and take not your holy Spirit from me.
>
> Give me the joy of your saving help again and sustain me with your bountiful Spirit.

I shall teach your ways to the wicked, and sinners shall
return to you.

Deliver me from death, O God, and my tongue shall
sing of your righteousness, O God of my salvation.[112]

Some have seen a kind of stubbornness in this *sermon* of Francis.
It is regarded by some scholars of the last century as something
akin to the "anti-sermon"—and that may be true inasmuch
as Francis emphasized a different sort of preaching. This was
a dramatic example of preaching with one's life. To live a life
according to Psalm 51 is not to speak about it but to do it, as
Francis demonstrated. One of the messages of the ashes sermon
was undoubtedly that there is an essence to the Christian life that
can easily become lost among traditions of formal learning and
formal practices of worship (such as preaching and listening),
and that this essence is experienced in contrition, the most basic
response to Christ.

But there is another, deeper way of understanding the ashes
sermon. All great spiritual teachers, both Christian and not, have
used silence to communicate the essence of faith. At the end of
his life, the prolific Indian poet Rabindranath Tagore said that
"languagelessness" was more important than poetry, and he then
tried (ironically) to capture the spirit of silence in his final verses.
Sometimes, it is what is *not* said that is of the utmost importance.
Regardless of the medium, there is something utterly basic about
silence as we relate to the divine, and yet we so easily miss it.

Francis's ashes sermon should remind us of when Jesus was
confronted by a group of scribes and Pharisees in the temple.
They brought to him a woman caught having sex with a man
other than her husband. They asked Jesus, who had previously

angered many Jewish leaders by teaching amendments to the law of Moses, saying that the law orders them to stone the woman: "What have you got to say?" they asked him (John 8:5). Jesus responded with silence. The next verse reads, "But Jesus bent down and started writing on the ground with his finger."

The ashes sermon may also remind us of what, in Buddhist tradition, is regarded as the Buddha's most important sermon. This is known as the flower sermon. In the fifth and sixth centuries BC, the Buddha was born in India and later died in China. Toward the end of his life, he gathered his followers together and delivered this memorable *talk*; but instead of speaking, he held up a flower. He held a lotus for many minutes without saying a word. The Buddha's followers were all confused and looked at each other. Some of them began to speak, trying to explain the purpose of the flower, its origins, its relationship to the tenets of religion. But it was only when one of them smiled, looking back at Buddha with understanding and obvious acceptance of this simple but dramatic gesture of serenity and peace and silence, that Buddha knew who would be the one to carry on his teachings. The tradition says that Buddha responded to that one, saying, "What can be said I have said to the others, but what cannot be said, I have given to you." I think that we need to understand Francis's ashes sermon in that same context: it was the occasion of Francis's passing on his teachings to Clare, who must have understood perfectly.[113]

Throughout her religious life, Clare lived behind the walls and iron grille of San Damiano that separated the first Franciscan women from the outside world. It was through that grille of intersecting iron bars that the women would receive the Eucharist from the hands of the brothers. We often get the sense that she wanted to be out and about more often with Francis and the friars, doing things that Sisters of St. Clare sometimes do today, but that were not really possible for religious women in the thirteenth century. The cloister remained her only home for more than forty years. But the world came to Clare. Bishops, cardinals, and popes were known to visit her in person at San Damiano in order to listen to her heavenly conversation. And since the early days of her ministry with Francis, when he and the friars would daily send the sick to San Damiano to be blessed by Clare and the sisters, the Poor Clares had been recognized for the heavenly power of their prayers.

The body of Francis came to Clare just after his death. Clare and the sisters could not be there when he died, as they stayed behind their iron grille, but the procession into Assisi brought Francis's body to them. Bonaventure tells us that the friars set down the body and stayed at San Damiano for quite a while, and the sisters both saw it and embraced it. The grille was removed. Biographer Paul Sabatier wrote: "In one of the frescos of the Upper Church in Assisi, Giotto has represented St. Clare and her companions coming out from San Damiano all in tears to kiss their spiritual father's corpse as it is being carried to its last home. With an artist's liberty he has made the chapel a rich church built of precious marbles."[114]

When Clare cried over the body of her good friend, her grief was probably increased by worry for what was happening to the movement they had founded. Elias and Cardinal Ugolino, who had been appointed by the pope to look after the young Franciscan Order, were slowly and deliberately steering things away from Francis's original *Rule*. And then, Cardinal Ugolino was elected Pope Gregory IX less than six months after the death of Francis. Clare's struggles to keep to the ideals deepened.

"Almost everything that was done in the Order after 1221 was done either without Francis's knowledge or against his will," explains Sabatier.[115] And the same was true for Clare in those final years.

The friars then left San Damiano en route to the church of San Giorgio (now a chapel within the Basilica of St. Clare in Assisi,) where Brother Elias had arranged for the funeral and burial. But the body would not rest at San Giorgio for long. On April 29, 1228, Pope Gregory IX issued a papal decree, or bull, announcing his intention to build a *specialis ecclesia*, "special church," to honor Francis. Less than eighteen months after the body was buried at San Giorgio, Elias acquired the land on the northwestern edge of Assisi known as the Hill of Hell, where thieves and murderers were often executed and then buried, and plans were underway to

On the third of October, 1226, St. Francis began his final agony, and after having the Canticle of the Creatures chanted to him once more he breathed his last. It is the great privilege of saints and poets that death opens for them even on earth a new life, for before the time of mourning is past, the glorious dead begin to excite the world, their words and example serving to incite generation to generation of disciples to interpret and imitate them. So, in order to be just to them, one must not only credit their lives and the works that they have left to us, but also with the followers they have inspired.

The poetic mission of St. Francis, eclipsed by other cares during his lifetime, never shone more brightly than in the century after his death. He had chosen for himself a burial-place on a hill to the east of Assisi called the Hill of Hell, where criminals were executed. But they had no sooner laid him in the tomb than an irresistible thrill stirred the world and became the inspiration of many minds. Pope Gregory IX placed him among the saints and decreed that his resting-place should be called the Hill of Paradise. From that time no honors were too great for this humble saint. People remembered his love for them, and wished to reward him richly for all the sacrifices he had made on their behalf.

Although he had had neither shelter nor servant, they built for him a magnificent resting-place like the palace he had dreamed of in his youth, where all types of artists might soon enter into his service. The rock had to be hollowed out to an unusual depth in order to protect the body from the risk of those thefts of relics which were so frequent in medieval times. Immediately over the tomb they erected a basilica to receive the crowd of pilgrims, and over that again they erected a second one from which prayers might ascend more quickly to heaven.

transform the land to the glory of St. Francis.

The unrepentant and the heretic could not, according to medieval laws, be buried in holy ground. That is why a place such as the Hill of Hell existed in most medieval towns. Bodies of those who were outside the Church needed to be buried somewhere. Ironically, there was no corresponding law against burying a good Christian in an unclean place. The Hill of Hell was unknown by firsthand experience to most Assisans, and was a place of frightening legends to the children of the town. That Francis would choose such a location for his burial was perfectly in keeping with his desire to be regarded as the lowliest of all before God. It was also a final act of solidarity with Christ, who died among thieves.

During the medieval era, many peasants, saints, and even kings would give much thought to how they should appear before the judgment seat of Christ after death. The belief was that a dead person, body and soul, would go directly to judgment, to face the question of one's eternal destiny. It was important to make the right impression. Once a fate was announced, he or she would go to heaven or hell, or perhaps, purgatory. Even the sixteenth-century Emperor Maximilian I, who was no great saint, left instructions that his body should be burned, his teeth smashed in, and his head shaved upon death. Despite what his earthly record might show, he wanted to at least seem physically penitent when he appeared before God.[116]

A northern architect, Jacopo Tedesco, came to build this double edifice, and applied to it all of the resources of Gothic art, all the traditions of Christian symbolism. He designed the lower basilica in the form of a solid nave without ornament, with arcades and openings that admit only a dim light, as if to recall the life of penitence of St. Francis on earth. He built the upper church with thinner walls, with bold arches, and with long windows through which the light streams in, as if to represent the glorious life of St. Francis in heaven.

—Frederick Ozanam

Gregory and Elias would honor Francis's request of burial site, but not according to the spirit of Francis's wishes. Elias was named the architect of the new basilica. Three months later, the same week that Francis was solemnly canonized by Gregory IX in a ceremony at San Giorgio, the first stone was ceremonially laid for the Lower Church of the new basilica. Gregory IX himself laid the stone, and the Hill of Hell was renamed the Hill of Paradise.

A new church building of the magnitude of the Basilica of Saint Francis in Assisi was never undertaken lightly. This solemn place was seen as a new tabernacle of Moses, a divine place where God would dwell in a special way with his people. It was a symbol of the New Jerusalem but, more literally, also as a gate to heaven. And it was built on the foundation of Francis of Assisi. Within two years, the Lower Church was completed and Francis's body moved there, and then within six additional years, the Upper Church was constructed, later to be adorned with priceless frescos by Giotto and others depicting the lives of Francis and his brothers, including an image of Elias himself kneeling before a crucifix.

The building of the basilica was one of the greatest architectural and artistic achievements of the Middle Ages. There is no denying the tremendous gifts that Elias possessed for architecture and organization. Gregory IX honored him by declaring through a papal bull that the basilica was now the mother church for all Franciscans, a title that had previously been used by the Poverello for the "little portion," Portiuncula, according to the *Mirror of Perfection*. All of this disgusted that handful of Franciscans who had been closest to Francis.

In the General Chapter meetings of 1230, the year that Elias completed the Lower Church, he maneuvered himself into position to be elected minister-general of the Order. But he failed, and another friar, John Parenti, was elected instead. For the next two years, Elias dedicated himself to constructing a shrine for Francis and turning Assisi into a place of pilgrimage that would rival Jerusalem and Compostela.

The body was buried in the Lower Church deep into the stone wall of its foundation. One writer has described the immense piece of rock that had stood in the middle of the Hill of Hell before the basilica was built—"an isolated rock surrounded on three sides by sharply falling precipices, and only joined to the city by a narrow neck of land almost cut through by a ravine which at the present day is filled up and built over by the upper and lower piazzas of San Francesco"—and it is probably into this foundation that the relic was securely entombed.[117]

A ceremony was planned, and guests invited, for the transferal of the body from San Giorgio to San Francesco. It requires about fifteen minutes to walk this distance today, and a procession would have taken well over an hour. But as the friars, honored guests, and townspeople all realized upon arriving at the basilica, the body was not there. Elias had arranged to have it secretly buried a few days earlier for fear that the crowd would tear it apart for relics.

The absence of a grave marker was not in itself unusual. Grave markers were uncommon in the thirteenth century, as the purpose of burial was not to commemorate a person as much as it was to add one to the community of believers. Anonymous burials in a common place of consecrated ground such as a chapel or parish were the norm. Even those clergy and religious who were buried inside a church were usually done so in unmarked spaces.[118] But still, Elias and the friars were afraid of the body being stolen by relic hunters. They hid it. The body was entombed into rock in such a way that exactly where it was remained a mystery for nearly six hundred years. Only in 1818 would a pope give permission to find the body and rebury it in the crypt of the basilica.

RESCUING THE SEPULCHER

As Elias and Pope Gregory were transforming the landscape of Assisi and organizing the Franciscan Order, Clare continued to play a leadership role on the spiritual side of the movement, but from a distance and from her cloister. It is believed that certain of the brothers—those who saw themselves in a direct line from Francis's earliest spiritual intentions—came to visit Clare and the sisters often, hearing confessions and administering the Eucharist, among other things. While he was still alive, Francis had actually warned the friars from visiting the sisters too often, but after his death they needed to reconnect with what united them.

These friars came to be known as "Spirituals," because they felt a strong connection to the original *Rule* of St. Francis and its emphasis on living strictly according to the Gospels. They would later fight bitterly, sometimes with deadly consequences, with the leaders of the Order and with the papacy in ways that would have saddened Francis and Clare. Brothers such as Leo, Angelo, Rufinus, Giles, Juniper, Bernard, and Masseo all lived to grieve for Brother Francis, and also for the integrity of their life. Elias and the others were replacing dancing with processions. They turned simplicity and humility into grandeur for the newly canonized. In their hands, the wildness of evangelical poverty and preaching was becoming tame and organized.

The friars surrounding Clare, and many of those scattered about, probably wanted to rescue Francis's sepulcher from Elias, and from those who would use pomp and riches to honor a saint who would have wanted nothing of it. The Spirituals would rather have been fools than churchmen. The ministers who followed Elias co-opted Francis's life and legacy for their causes, which included fundraising, building cathedrals, and devising intellectual systems that would endanger the Poverello's single-minded passion for firsthand experience. Elias and others were sincere in their reasons for building upon the foundation that had been laid by Francis and Clare, but there is no question that gone with Francis was the original movement he had founded.

CHAPTER 13

BURNING BOOKS

The story of Brother Francis and Sister Clare is replete with books and their reactions to books. Francis loved to use them for prayer, as we know from the early texts. He took books with him while traveling so that he could read the prayer offices while on the road. He began his religious life by turning to ornate books of Gospels and other texts from the bishop's library, but then later fought with friars who wanted to possess books of their own.

As the First and Second Orders filled rapidly with men and women of promising potential, many of them were ambitious, smart, and thoughtful. They heard Francis preach that learning and study and books were possessions no less dangerous to a holy life than were money and pride. He told them again and again that a friar or a sister needed simplicity and poverty more than books, but many of them didn't quite believe it. How could a preacher preach well without study, they wondered. Why must a joy-filled life exclude books and learning? The problems were very practical ones. In order to study, one needs books and leisure time. Stability also becomes important for a student, requiring ongoing access to libraries and teachers. All of these things were beside the point of faithfulness to Christ in the worldview of Francis and Clare.

On one memorable occasion, Francis pleaded with a young friar who wanted to own his own breviary. Francis was trying to teach the friars that prayer books were for changing one's life, not for owning, but by the time of this encounter, he was no longer the minister-general. Nevertheless, the young friar persisted in asking for Francis's blessing to own one. Francis wouldn't give it, but instead, pleaded with the boy to become a passionate follower of Christ who doesn't need to own anything. He shouted, "*I* am a breviary! *I* am a breviary!"

Some of the most beloved books of the first Franciscans were actually about Francis. Thomas of Celano's *First Life* was circulated the year after canonization (in 1229), and his *Second Life* about eighteen years later (in 1246 or 1247). These volumes looked little like our books of today, except that they were usually taller than they were wide, and similar in size to today's books. They were hand copied, as this was the era before the printing press, and usually made of vellum, a prepared animal skin. This made some books very sturdy and rigid, while others could become greasy. Few books in those days were of one text only. There was no such thing as copyright law, and books were all custom-made. A biography of St. Francis might also include a litany of the saints, the little Office of the Virgin, a collection of penitential psalms, an anonymous treatise on the Apocalypse, and a prayer to the patron saint of the book's owner.

We also know that Thomas's two biographies of Francis circulated outside of the friaries and were among the most popular books of the day. Since Francis was believed to be a saint even before his death and his canonization was decisively swift, the stories about him were quickly assumed into the already popular genre of devotional literature known as the

lives of the saints. Numerous First, Second, and Third Order
Franciscans joined because of having read Thomas of Celano's
accounts. The same has happened in subsequent eras: Carmelite
convents were flooded with young women in the decades after
Therese of Lisieux's *Story of a Soul* was first published at the
end of the nineteenth century, and Thomas Merton's Abbey
of Gethsemani was bursting at the seams in the late 1940s
and early 1950s as young men came back from World War II
and read Merton's autobiography *The Seven Storey Mountain*,
finding the meaning to their lives.

Given all of this, it must have been especially difficult for the
friars to obey an order in 1266 to destroy all copies of Thomas of
Celano's biographies of Francis.

Bonaventure wrote his *Life* of Francis at the commission of the
General Chapter meeting of 1260. He wanted to bring peace
to the factions that were tearing apart the Order. Details were
added that enhanced the legend of Francis as the founder of a
brilliant new movement. Bonaventure's book represented no new
research or insight, but rather a beautiful retelling of Thomas of
Celano's stories without references to the loss of spiritual ideals.
It is simply a redaction, which is why it is unfortunate that today
Bonaventure's is by far the most read of the early biographies of
Francis.

At the General Chapter of 1266, Bonaventure and the Franciscans
declared that all earlier biographies of St. Francis were to be
destroyed. The resolution reads:

> The General Chapter commands likewise in the name
> of obedience, that all legends that have been written about
> St. Francis shall be destroyed, and where they are found

outside the Order, the Brothers will seek to dispose of them, because the legend which was written by the General is made up of what he heard from their mouths, who were with St. Francis nearly all the time and knew everything with certainty.[119]

No stories have come down to us of massive book burnings in the friaries or convents, but no doubt, there were some strident friars and sisters who stoked fires in places like Siena, Bologna, and Florence. We know very little about how books were destroyed and how many. We can imagine that many copies were buried rather than burned, as it was the medieval tradition to bury a holy book in order to dispose of it, as a show of respect. Still other copies were hidden away from the eyes of those who desired them destroyed. Meanwhile, the Spirituals were soon to begin collecting and writing down the stories of Francis and Clare that became *The Little Flowers*. The loss of Thomas of Celano's accounts made pulling together other texts all the more important.

A battle was not just brewing; it was already underway for the heart of the movement. Nowhere do we see this tension as clearly as we do in *The Mirror of Perfection*. In the tenth tale, for example, Francis is depicted as counseling his brothers how to build a house and church upon settling in a new city. It is impossible to read this tale today without seeing the hand of a later editor at work, using comments of Francis to dispute the leaders of his Order after his death. Francis's comments about the building of churches must have been intended to counter the extravagance of the new Basilica of St. Francis just built in Assisi by Brother Elias:

And let them make little churches, for they ought not to have great churches built, neither for the sake of preaching to the people nor upon another occasion, for the humility is greater and the example better when they go to other churches to preach. . . . Many a time do the brethren have great buildings made, breaking thereby our holy poverty, giving occasion of mischievous whispers, and setting a bad example unto many.

Similarly, as we mentioned above, the editors of *The Mirror* quote Francis as saying that Portiuncula, "as the smallest and poorest church," should always remain "the head and mother of the poor Friars Minor." The fifty-fifth tale even quotes Francis as saying, "The Lord wishes that no other church should be given to the friars, and that the friars should not build a new church."

Despite the Spirituals' best efforts to change things back to where they had been, the movement was formalizing in ways that were supported by the majority of the friars and sisters and by Rome. Bonaventure understood that changes had to be made in order for the Franciscans to enter a new, post-Francis era of productivity and growth. Never mind that those were not virtues in the mind of their founder, and the Franciscans of the generation after Francis believed that what had begun simply and with purity should naturally develop into something more defined and sustainable. At one point, Bonaventure makes this clear, as he defends the lack of book learning among the first followers of Francis:

It should not disturb you that the first brothers were simple and illiterate. On the contrary, that should confirm your faith in the Order. I confess before God that this is what most made me love the life of Blessed Francis—that it was like the beginning and perfection of the church itself, which began first among simple fishermen and later progressed into the most renowned and learned doctors. . . . That this was a divine work is demonstrated by the fact that the learned did not refuse to join the company of such simple men.[120]

With Bonaventure's rule as minister-general, and the changes that were happening in step with it, Francis and Clare became saints to revere more than life examples to imitate. Many of the principles of Francis's original *Rule* faded away or were taken far less literally, and those who dissented from these majority opinions were marginalized.

THE INFLUENCE OF BROTHER ELIAS

Francis loved Elias, that we know. Three years after Francis's death, Thomas of Celano recorded that Elias was "the one he chose to be as a mother to himself, and also as a father to the other brothers." Elias was the only one able to insist that Francis take medicine to alleviate pain, when others had failed. Francis appointed him as minister to the all-important province of the Holy Land, and then later visited him there just after abdicating his leadership of the Order. Elias was one of the privileged few to have seen up close and firsthand the wounds of Christ imprinted on the saint's body, two years before his death. And Thomas wrote of Francis's deathbed, saying, "There was a brother there whom Francis loved with the greatest affection," which was most likely Elias.[121] Clare also praised Elias in her second letter to Blessed Agnes of Prague. Clare urged Agnes to "follow the advice of our honorable father, Brother Elias, the minister-general, so that you will walk safely in the way of the Lord."

In the election .of 1232, Elias succeeded John Parenti and was elected to the post of minister-general. His work of protecting the body of Francis and building Assisi into a palace of pilgrimage was largely over. But by 1239, after Clare's letter was written to Agnes, Elias had been deposed by the pope at the overwhelming demand of the friars. Salimbene tells us that Elias, once one of Francis's trusted advisors and friends, turned against his own brothers after the founder's death. Elias was the leader of those who would expand the role of the friars in the world, welcoming the ownership of property, the cultivation of learning, and the building of splendid churches and monuments—including the Basilica of St. Francis in Assisi. Salimbene no doubt felt betrayed by Elias as well, as it was Elias who received young Salimbene as a postulant and sheltered him from his angry father (who wanted to thwart the conversion) while Elias was minister-general.[122] But Elias's independence was combined with excessive pride and a lust for increasing influence.

When he was finally deposed as minister-general, Elias rebelled by joining up with the excommunicated Holy Roman Emperor Frederick II, who was at war with the pope. He took some friars with him in this fight, and the reputation of the Order was seriously damaged. Salimbene recounts that "I myself have heard a hundred times" the singing of a little ditty by the Umbrian peasants whenever a friar would pass by during this time, "Frater Elias is gone astray / And hath taken the evil way." Salimbene says: "At the sound of this song, the good brothers were cut to the heart." By the time Thomas of Celano wrote his *Second Life* of Francis in 1246–1247, Elias had been disgraced and is not mentioned by name.

14

THE RISE AND FALL
OF THE SPIRITUALS

Prophets are supposed to make religious leaders nervous. They challenge the status quo and attempt to incite people to change their ways. When Francis and Clare insisted on absolute poverty for themselves and their followers, this always rankled the popes and cardinals who were assigned to look after them. The situation may remind us of what it was like in Jesus' last week in Jerusalem before the Passion, when religious fervor was everywhere and was stimulated easily by passing prophets and teachers. Like the church in Francis's time, the synagogue in Christ's time was interested in settling matters of doctrine and practices of faith and organizing religious activities and tithes under the umbrella of those good teachings and works. In other words, organized religion has always preferred to remain organized, and the Catholic Church in the days of Francis and Clare was no different from organized faith anytime, anywhere. Preaching lives of voluntary poverty was subversive to these ends. How would the people tithe to the church if they had no money? Would they even come to services if they were following an itinerant preacher? Francis practiced a peripatetic faith that did not lend itself easily to settled communities of faithful churchgoers.

Francis experienced skepticism about his unorganized band of followers from the very beginning, when they visited Pope Innocent III in Rome. Innocent III hesitated before granting approval to Francis for his young movement. He wanted to be sure that they were properly organized and that they took on characteristics of a true religious order. To that end, he made sure that the twelve of them were tonsured, marked as religious at least by their visible haircuts, before leaving Rome. And he deliberated long before sanctioning the sort of poverty that the Poverello insisted upon, trying first to persuade him otherwise.

Pope Honorius III later hesitated as well before approving Francis's revised *Rule*. Honorius, in fact, persuaded the saint to remove a clause that would permit friars to follow a literal interpretation of the *Rule*, even if their future ministers objected.[123] A few years later, Pope Gregory IX had brought about additional changes to the original vision, revising Francis's teachings on poverty even further. Two or three years before Francis died, the quotation from Luke's Gospel—"Take nothing for the journey: neither staff, nor haversack, nor bread, nor money; and do not have a spare tunic"—was removed from the *Rule* despite Francis's objections. It was no longer deemed prudent to expect that all friars would or could follow such an instruction to the letter. The *Rule* of 1223 is, in fact, changed from the original vision in many ways. The overall effect was the slowing of the gospel of Franciscanism. Brothers were no longer called "Friars Minor," which literally means "Lesser Brothers," a name instituted by Francis as a description of their poverty; they were permitted to ride rather than walk; and poverty began to take on spiritual rather than literal meanings. The idealism of Francis and Clare was giving way to something much more familiar.

Francis's body was already falling apart at this time, in 1223. The next year, he made his monthlong retreat on Alverno, which really sapped his energies and by which time he was almost blind and crippled. When he finally left the mountain, Francis was forced to ride a donkey rather than walk. It is on this occasion, as they traveled through various towns en route back to Assisi, that Francis was recognized as a living saint in the eyes of the people. "*Santo, santo,*" they called him, in those last years of his life. They touched him, snatched pieces of his clothing, and followed him, sensing the vanishing presence of a unique man.

His detractors said nothing out loud at this time; it was clear to all that Francis was dying. He would spend more time preaching, the familiar voice but without the usual vitality, and he would be for a while at San Damiano in Clare's care. The time to continue *normalizing* the Order was close at hand for Gregory IX and Elias.

The opponents of Francis and Clare thought that he and his most energetic followers were reckless. Imagine a group of reforming Christians who refuse to own anything, decline opportunities for comfort or schooling, and who refuse to plan for the future or even to take good physical care of themselves. Established communities have persecuted groups that fit one or more of these characterizations for centuries. According to the Franciscan Spirituals, Christians without such a literal commitment to the teachings of Jesus were consumed instead by a "worldly prudence and caution."[124] Meanwhile, their detractors called the Spirituals fools, and they didn't mean this as a compliment. The conflict was between order and chaos, and the Spirituals preferred chaos. Miguel de Unamuno was accused of a similar sort of foolishness in the last century, and he responded sarcastically: "No—nothing that is regulated and contained and channeled and directed by graduates, curates, barbers, canons, and dukes is fanaticism. Nothing that flies a banner proclaiming logical formulas, nothing that has a program, nothing that offers a plan for tomorrow which an orator can expound in a methodical fashion, is fanaticism."[125]

Which excess would you prefer? For the Spirituals, the choice was an easy one: an excess of faithfulness to Francis and Clare and to Christ.

The name *Spirituals* is actually a misnomer when applied to the beliefs of any Franciscan before the fourteenth century, for it appears that the term did not exist until about that time. But to understand the name, it is necessary to travel back in time to an earlier prophet who inspired Francis, Joachim of Fiore. Paul Sabatier summarizes the life of the enigmatic, traveling ascetic:

> Converted after a life of dissipation, Joachim of Fiore traveled extensively in the Holy Land, Greece, and Constantinople. Returning to Italy he began, though a layman, to preach in the outskirts of Rende and Cosenza. Later on he joined the Cistercians . . . and there took vows. Shortly after being elected abbot of the monastery in spite of refusal and even flight, he was seized after a few years with the nostalgia of solitude, and sought from Pope Lucius III a discharge from his functions (1181). . . . Then began for Joachim a life of wandering from monastery

to monastery that carried him even as far as Lombardy. . . . When he returned to the south, a group of disciples gathered around him to hear his explanations of the most obscure passages of the Bible . . . in the very heart of the Sila, the Black Forest of Italy. . . . This new Athos received the name of Fiore (flower), transparent symbol of the hopes of its founder.[126]

Joachim's interpretation of history prevailed in the minds of the early Franciscans. He divided the history of humanity into three periods. The first period he called the reign of God the Father; this was a time when people lived under the law and the threat of punishment for failing to keep the law. The second period was the reign of God the Son, when grace was brought to troubled humanity and humanity was taught to be obedient in a new way, as kin or family. And the third period—believed by the Spirituals to be the period into which they were presently entering—was the reign of God the Spirit. This third era was to be characterized by love and freedom triumphing over fear and law.

With this prophetic understanding, the true spirit of what became known as the Spirituals began way back when Francis and his first followers were staying in the caves of Carceri, tending to lepers, and during the time that they lived loosely around Portiuncula, working in the fields during the day, preaching in the churches, begging for their bread, and sleeping under the stars at night. In those very things was the essence of the movement, according to Francis. He wrote in his *Testament*, his last and greatest work, that the friars should always be "strangers and pilgrims" in their observance of poverty without property and possessions.

At the same time, it is easy to understand why some of the followers who came soon after this golden period wanted much more, and believed that God wanted more for the Franciscans, too. Ironically, Francis's idealism drew not only thousands of men to the First Order, but also some of the most talented and intellectual men of the day. More ironic, still: these men would not remain satisfied with humility and mendicancy. They would become influential scholars and powerful clerics, and would build grand churches such as the basilica in Assisi and Santa Croce in Florence. They built churches; they built schools; they developed massive libraries; they sent the smarter friars off to university in Paris and Rome and elsewhere; they sent emissaries—not just on mission trips—but to visit with cardinals and popes and protectors throughout the civilized world. The Spirituals wanted none of this. They wanted things to remain as they were in the early days with Francis and Clare. To them, there was little difference between the *Rule* of St. Francis and the Gospels themselves; that is, in fact, how Francis intended it.

Beginning at about the time of Francis's death, the ministers of the Order began to take firmer control. The dissension that eventually led to the separation of Conventuals from Spirituals began even in Francis's own lifetime. He resigned as leader of the Order and changes began to take place. The Order was growing into something that was too large for him to lead simply by the force of his charismatic teaching and personality. We even see scenes in which Francis, at the end of his life, was pleading for permission to speak to gathered assemblies of Franciscans.

After Francis's death, it was the papacy of Gregory IX that really heated up the debates. Gregory listened carefully to those ministers who wanted to make changes. On the other side were Brother

Leo and his followers, who insisted that the words of Francis's *Testament* be enforced. In the *Testament*, Francis wrote very clearly that there should be no other rule for Franciscan life than the *Rule* that he wrote, and also that his *Testament* would provide any commentary on the *Rule* that was necessary. Gregory IX ruled controversially after Francis's death that the *Testament* did not have any legal authority on the Order because it had never been formally approved by the ministers.

Prominent among the Spirituals after the deaths of Francis and Clare were the friars Leo, Angelo, and Giles, but the minister-general at that time, John of Parma, was also sympathetic. A priest and professor of theology, he was the sort of Franciscan that the Conventuals could easily understand, but yet the texts tell us that he aided the Spirituals' cause by removing restrictions that had been put upon them. John of Parma held office from 1247 until 1257, when it is most likely that he was urged to resign by Pope Alexander IV. Bonaventure was then elected minister-general, and he tried John of Parma in a doctrinal court for heretically adhering to the teachings of Joachim of Fiore. Eventually, John was acquitted and retired to a hermitage.

Ubertino of Casale (d. 1329) led the embattled Spirituals into the fourteenth century. He is the monk made famous by Umberto Eco in his novel *The Name of the Rose*. Late in life, he became known as a grizzled veteran of spiritual and political battles within the Order. There is a touching scene from 1285 when Ubertino visited the aging John of Parma at his hermitage in Greccio, the place memorable for the reenacted Nativity that Francis created with real people and animals. Like John, Ubertino became a champion of the ideas of Joachim of Fiore and wrote a lengthy work applying Joachim's historiography to his present situation.

The Nativity of St. Francis

The Spirituals did not always stand on solid, reasonable ground in their disputes with the leaders of their order, and the papal schism of the early fourteenth century (when two or three competing popes were ruling simultaneously, sometimes excommunicating each other) only confused the situation further. Like Joachim of Fiore, Ubertino strove to demonstrate how then-current events fit God's prophetic plans. He believed that Elijah prefigured Christ, and that Christ prefigured Francis of Assisi. He was enthralled with the Apocalypse of St. John. We shouldn't trust this sort of enthusiasm. We have good reasons, in fact, to be suspicious of any Christian who has a strong attachment to the book of Revelation. Nothing good has ever come of such speculation. Instead, wars have begun, passions enflamed that run counter to the teachings of Christ, and endless theological debates. We shouldn't trust Ubertino's prophetic comparisons of the anti-Christ in Revelation 13 to Pope Boniface VIII any more than we trust such comparisons to figures in our own day.

The first effort of the Spirituals to really organize came in the days just after the death of Bonaventure, in 1274, at the Council of Lyon that year. Their leadership came from that area of Italy known as the Marches of Ancona, a region where many of them were living in relative seclusion, safe from the Conventuals, who occasionally wanted to do them harm. It was in the Marches that the Spirituals preserved the oral tradition of the tales of Francis's life known as the *Fioretti*: "The province of the Marches of Ancona was once full of holy men shining like lights from heaven. Their holy, resplendent example filled the skies as stars illuminate the world on a dark night."[127] In fact, there were not only holy *men* in the Marches—there were holy *women*, as well. Most scholars believe that the first convent of Poor Clares outside of Assisi was founded there when an entire convent of Benedictine women asked for permission to join the movement founded at San Damiano.

It would not be long, however, before the Conventuals would tolerate the Spirituals no longer. Religious truth was taken very seriously in the late Middle Ages in ways that are difficult to understand today, and monastic obedience was an equally serious matter. The Conventuals believed that obedience was more important than any other virtue in a friar, and the Spirituals were disobedient sons who needed to be punished in order to learn the truth. Obedience could even be beaten into someone, if necessary.

15

AFTER CLARE'S DEATH

C lare had been alluding to her impending death for months by the time she lay dying in a small corner of San Damiano. Thomas of Celano tells us that she was looking forward to death so that she could meet the poor Christ whom she loved so much. It was the summer of 1253, exactly twenty-seven years after her friend, Francis, had gone through his own preparations for death.

Clare knew that she would die. In the days before modern science and medicine, it was far more common to wither away slowly from disease than it was to die of a massive coronary or be trampled by an oxcart. Clare called for one of the friars to come and hear her confession and give her Communion, and it appears that it was Brother Reginald who came first. Other friars came too, and she asked them to recite various passages from Scripture, probably the penitential psalms, and then the psalm that Francis had prayed just before his own death, number 142:

> I cry to the Lord with my voice;
>> to the Lord I make loud supplication.
> I pour out my complaint before him
>> and tell him all my trouble.

When my spirit languishes within me, you know my path;

in the way wherein I walk they have hidden a trap for me.

I look to my right hand and find no one who knows me;

I have no place to flee to, and no one cares for me.

I cry out to you, O LORD;

I say, "You are my refuge,

my portion in the land of the living."

Listen to my cry for help, for I have been brought very low;

save me from those who pursue me,

for they are too strong for me.

Bring me out of prison, that I may give thanks to your Name;

when you have dealt bountifully with me,

the righteous will gather around me.[128]

Thomas tells us that when Clare saw Brother Juniper among the friars, she asked him to speak his eloquent parables and witty sayings, teaching her again with reminders of Franciscan beauty, joy, and foolishness. His words so moved her that she turned to the sisters and reminded them of their vows and the promises of their calling. Medieval deathbed penitents were often advised by their clergy to look at a cross on the wall, or to simply lie on their backs and look up to heaven, and to fear death. But Clare was not afraid; she wanted death to come, and Juniper had reminded her why.

Clare was mindful of the young but troubled movement she would be leaving behind. We also know that Angelo and Leo were there at her deathbed, along with many of the sisters. They were Spirituals, and of one mind with Clare about the future of their way of living. She was the most important disciple of the one who first inspired her—and all of Italy—to joy and faith and a renewal of the bond between humanity and creation. Francis had burst onto the parched religious scene half a century before, and after two decades of meteoric spiritual growth and enlightenment, his movement had been waylaid by controversy, dissension, and scandal. And now, there lay Clare. Together with only a handful of others, she represented another ending of an era of faithfulness to the original ideals.

An Austrian artist known to history as the Master of Heiligenkreuz painted a scene of Clare's deathbed in about 1400 that accentuated the mystical. The remarkable painting hangs now in The National Gallery of Art in Washington, D.C., and depicts the vision of Sister Benvenuta, one of Clare's original followers, as she testified at the hearings for Clare's canonization. Benvenuta saw her spiritual mother surrounded on her deathbed by the Virgin Mary and various virgin martyrs. In the vision and in the painting, St. Mary supports Clare's head, comforting her, while St. Barbara, St. Margaret of Antioch, St. Catherine of Alexandria, and St. Agnes of Rome stand all around.[129] In addition to psalms, it would be surprising if Clare's sisters had not sung the Salve Regina to honor the Virgin Mary at the death of this virgin soon-to-be saint:

Hail, holy Queen, mother of Mercy!
Our life, our sweetness, and our hope!
To thee do we cry, poor banished
children of Eve, to thee do we send
up our sighs, mourning and weeping
   in this valley of tears.
Turn, then, most gracious advocate,

thine eyes of mercy toward us; and
after this our exile show unto us the
blessed fruit of thy womb, Jesus;
O clement, O loving, O sweet Virgin Mary.
Pray for us, O holy Mother of God
that we may be made worthy of the
promises of Christ.

Just before passing away, Clare began speaking quietly to herself, saying, "Go forth, go forth, you are blessed and created by God." One of the sisters asked her who she was talking to, and Clare replied, "I am talking to my own happy soul!"

Clare had always wanted to stick to the ideals. Nothing else would do—for either the Poor Clares or for the other Franciscans who insisted on faithfulness to the original *Rule* of Francis. It is somewhat unfortunate that she took to calling herself Francis's *pianticella*, or "little plant," because she was much more than that. Bonaventure later built on Clare's self-declaration and referred to her as "the first flower in Francis' garden," which couldn't have meant the chronological first, but rather, the superlative first. Even so, I believe that these images diminish more than flatter her.

She had been given a great gift on her deathbed. Clare was the first woman in history to write her own *Rule* for religious life, and it was approved only two days before she died. The story of Clare composing her *Rule* is a story of tremendous courage and a testimony to the strength of her will. Before Clare, men wrote all of the rules for women. But she campaigned for the opportunity to compose her own for much of her religious life, and especially after the death of Francis. Preserving voluntary poverty in all areas was her goal. She wanted to be sure that the Poor Clares would own nothing, including the houses that they lived in, and rely entirely on the graciousness of the brothers to bring them what was necessary. In 1253, Pope Innocent IV granted approval for Clare's *Rule* that included these provisions. A few years earlier, he himself had insisted that the women relax their commitments, just as Pope Gregory IX had done in the years immediately following Francis's death. She kissed her *Rule* before she died, beside the place where the pope had signed it with his approval.

Clare's *Rule* would prove a disappointment to the true disciplinarians, however. The Dominican sisters, who were closest to the Poor Clares in many respects, had rules against laughing or making someone else laugh, eating without permission, and any subtle rebellion in word or deed. Penalties for breaking the rules were spelled out in detail. Flogging was a common form of discipline, and humiliating oneself by eating bread and water while kneeling before the rest of the community, a common penance. With its themes and emphases, Clare sent the message to her sisters and to the authorities who approve monastic rules not that Franciscans were not serious or strict—because Francis and Clare could be both—but that to be a Franciscan was a decision made each day, voluntarily, for Christ. The spiritual life is not a path of renunciations.

She died on August 11, 1253, and her body was buried, as Francis's had been, at San Giorgio. Two years later, on September 26, 1255, Clare was canonized by Pope Alexander IV, who had once been Clare's cardinal-protector but then succeeded Innocent IV as pope. In 1260, again like Francis, her body was transferred to the crypt of a great church built for her, the Basilica of St. Clare. The two basilicas face each other, one on either end of Assisi.

After Clare's death, the spirit of the age seems to have turned more and more away from the joy and freedom and charity that had defined the previous fifty years. Ominous events showed the waning of their spirit on the religious scene. There was, for instance, the rise of self-flagellation and the use of self-inflicted pain as a tool for spiritual understanding and commitment. The theologian Peter Damian had defended self-flagellation in the eleventh century but the practice did not become widespread until the middle of the thirteenth. Flagellants and others used pain as a vivid way of remembering what Christ did on the cross— and, more aptly—in the scourging he received on the way to the Cross.

The Flagellants became a group of like-minded and penitent laypeople in about 1260. Led by a hermit from Perugia, neighbor town to Assisi, they felt that they were atoning for their sins through public whippings, and their emotion seemed to match the era, which was full of war and conflict, plague and death. These groups of people appeared from town to town throughout what is now Italy, France, and Germany, and became especially prominent a century later when the plague, or Black Death, was at its height.

Franciscans also began to discriminate narrowly as to who would be admitted and who would not in the decades after Clare's death. Contrary to Francis's original vision of inclusiveness, Salimbene tells of the friaries judging on the basis of parentage, literacy, and seriousness—none of which were important in the early days. Some of those who were ultimately rejected by the Order on grounds such as these would periodically form their own makeshift groups in attempts to model themselves after the *real* Francis. The response of the Franciscans to these groups was to condemn them and to appeal to Rome to take measures toward the same. We actually see some of the first instances of what would later become known as litigating to prevent trademark infringement, as the ministers appealed to the pope to forbid any other organizations from copying the traditional Franciscan habit, sandals, and cord.

Theology took on greater importance as well. Within one year of Clare's death, the task of fighting heresy—known as the Inquisition—was transferred from the Dominicans to the Franciscans. The Dominicans were founded for the express purpose of fighting heresy, which is why the pope so quickly granted permission to young Dominic of Guzman's new order. The name Dominican (*Domini canes* in Latin) means literally "Hounds of the Lord." The early Dominicans commonly used force, fierce argument, and religious courts in order to combat those who held heretical beliefs within Christianity, and occasionally, non-Christians. Supported by the brilliant theological method of Thomas Aquinas and Albertus Magnus, two great Dominican theologians, they sought to solidify their theological system as the official one of the Church, and to argue its infallibility to those who might disagree.

Francis and Clare had had no stomach for these sorts of militant, theological arguments over orthodoxy; but after their passing, many of the Franciscans did. The transferring of Inquisition responsibilities was a way for Rome to place its support firmly against the Spirituals, who only wanted to continue the focus of Francis and Clare: Love over the sword, orthopraxy over orthodoxy. The hope of Dante's *Paradiso* would have made sense to them, but not the intimate characterizations of divine punishments and sentences of judgment in the *Inferno*. Dante wrote fifty-five years after Clare's death. A generation later, when the plague reached Umbria with terrifying force in 1348, many called it God's judgment. Francis and Clare never would have had such an idea, even though they came into contact with a tremendous amount of sickness and death. Essential evil was not a subject that they ever chose to think about. Until the end, their sole vocation remained loving rather than identifying or discussing what might be the opposite of love. Dante's final couplet from *Paradiso* fits perfectly as the voice of Francis and Clare:

My will and my desire were turned by love,
The love that moves the sun and other stars.[130]

KILLING THE SPIRITUALS

The series of events that brought an end to the breakaway movement of the Spirituals is one of the darkest in the history of Christianity. After Clare's death, the aim of the Spirituals was to obtain authorization for a separation from the Order. They insisted that they must have the right to practice their faith as they believed Francis himself would have them to do. Many of them, in fact, by this time in history had never once resided in a Conventual, or approved, Franciscan monastery. They were living completely outside the boundaries of the accepted Order. They wandered from town to town and preached, begged, and prayed, as Francis had done. They flourished— more in vehemence and emotion than in numbers—primarily in the Umbrian and Marches regions of Italy and also in southern France. But the divisions grew deeper and deeper. The Spirituals were more separated from the Conventuals than ever before, both geographically and religiously, and the Conventuals seemed to them to be completely lost. By 1292, for instance, a rule actually had to be passed that told friars to stop carrying knives and purses in their belts.[131]

For less than a year, from July to December of 1294, the Spirituals found a friend in Pope Celestine V. Celestine gave them permission to live in separated, small hermitages, similar to those that once surrounded the Portiuncula, and to practice Francis's *Rule* apart from any outside interpretations, from the papacy or elsewhere—a right that Francis himself had foreseen would likely be infringed upon as he wrote: "I, Brother Francis, firmly command and decree that no one delete or add to what has been written in this life. The brothers may have no other Rule."[132] These particular Spirituals formed another breakaway group from the larger, more disorganized Spirituals, and for a time took the name Celestine Friars, in honor of their champion pope, or Poor Hermits, a phrase of which Francis would only have approved the first half. There were splinter groups everywhere at this time, and Church authorities were becoming more and more impatient.

Celestine V had a hermit's disposition and a saintly personality. He was completely unsuited for the late medieval papacy and resigned in less than a year, the first man ever to do so. Within three days of his election in December of that year, the new Pope Boniface VIII rescinded every favor of leniency that Celestine had granted in his year in the chair of St. Peter. Many Spirituals fled to faraway places such as Greece and Sicily to both "withdraw from the brothers' wrath and . . . that they should retreat to . . . freely serve the Lord," according to Angelo Clareno, who took over the leadership of the Celestine Spirituals in 1305 and later wrote the history of the period.[133] The Spirituals then rejected Boniface VIII as pope, and were promptly (and understandably) excommunicated by him.

Boniface, meanwhile, chased down and imprisoned Celestine—employing soldiers to hunt him on foot through the woods of Apulia (Celestine simply wanted to find a quiet hermitage) and then by sea as the monk fled across the Adriatic in a boat—because Boniface was afraid that Celestine's sweetness and sympathies for the Spirituals could gain the appearance of ecclesiastical authority. A pope had never abdicated the throne before, and Boniface's paranoid mind feared that the people might not accept his resignation as easily as the College of Cardinals had done. In truth, Boniface—a skilled jurist and diplomat—had maneuvered and manipulated for the resignation and removal of the recluse Celestine. Eventually, the poor ex-pope washed ashore in the middle of the night as a result of a violent storm and landed back in Italy, at the village of Vieste on the tip of the Gargano peninsula, a beautiful place that is mostly national park today. Celestine would have liked to remain there in quiet, but instead was captured by Boniface's men and returned to Rome. He was brought before Boniface and then sentenced to exile in a castle near Rome, where he died less than a year later.

After Boniface, Clement V was elected to the chair of St. Peter in 1305. Like Celestine before him, Clement was at times lenient with the Spirituals and pleaded with them in France to find monasteries in which to reside, wanting to bring a peaceful end to the controversies surrounding observance. As a result of

Clement's peacemaking efforts, three Franciscan monasteries saw an influx of Spirituals return: at Beziers, Narbonne, and Carcassonne, all in the Languedoc region of France. But within a few years, when both Clement and a sympathetic Franciscan minister-general (Alexander of Alexandria) had died, Conventual superiors were again appointed at these convents, and the conflict really heated up. The Spirituals were booted from the three monasteries, and they responded by attempting to take two of them, Beziers and Narbonne, by force. This won them quick, fresh excommunications, but the Spirituals persisted, this time by peaceful means, taking their appeal to yet another General Chapter meeting of the Order, in Naples, Italy, in 1316. In the year following, then Pope John XXII, at the urging of minister-general Michael of Cesena, brought a number of the Spirituals' leaders, including Angelo Clareno and Ubertino of Casale, to appear before him in Avignon for a doctrinal trial. They were ordered to submit to authority or be excommunicated and burned at the stake. "Great is poverty, but greater is obedience," Pope John infamously said.

Twenty-five of these men were given over to an Inquisitor, who, according to the euphemistic language of the *Catholic Encyclopedia*, "succeeded in converting twenty-one of them," which means that they were threatened and tortured. The remaining four refused to acknowledge a religious authority higher than the original *Rule* of St. Francis, which they believed to be equivalent to the very gospel of Christ. These four were burned at the stake in Marseilles on May 7, 1318, a horrific day in the history of the Church and the Franciscan movement.

The two most prominent Spirituals were spared death at the hands of John XXII: Ubertino of Casale, because he was defended in Avignon before the papal court by a sympathetic cardinal, and Angelo Clareno, because he fled for his life. Any remaining Spirituals were further marginalized and resided with Angelo in one of the most remote and arid regions of Italy, Basilicata. It is there that lonely mountain peaks slide down into the Ionian Sea. These men were soon known as *Clareni*, because the Spirituals had been officially suppressed, and after Angelo himself died in 1337, we hear very little more of them.

LIGHT IN
THE DARK AGES

The most famous scene of Francis and Clare together must be the occasion of their "Holy Conversation." The occasion was alluded to in chapter 1 in the discussion of St. Benedict and St. Scholastica, and an image of that day can be seen on page *iv* of this book.

Francis had to be persuaded by his brothers to eat this special meal with Clare. For some reason, even though the texts say that Francis would often visit Clare at San Damiano, he was hesitant to sit down at table with her there. Perhaps he felt that the formality of it, or the preparations that would be made for it, were unnecessary. Nevertheless, this is one occasion when we see the friars chiding their founder. According to *The Little Flowers*, his companions said to him, "Father, it seems to us that you are being too strict in this instance, and not living according to the love that you preach. You should grant this simple request of Sister Clare, in so little a thing as having a meal with you."

He was persuaded and replied, "Since it seems so to you, I agree. But, let's make the meal even more enjoyable for Sister

Clare, and have it at St. Mary of the Angels [Portiuncula], for she has been cloistered for a long time. Besides, she will enjoy seeing that special place once again where she first became the spouse of Christ."

When Clare arrived that day, she first paid respect to the statue of the Blessed Virgin above the altar, and then the friars showed her around the place until dinner was ready. It had been several years since she had seen Portiuncula and the small compound of huts that had grown up around it. They all ate together on the bare ground, as Francis always preferred to do. During the first course, it is said that Francis began to speak about God in such a way that the whole place was filled with light. Clare listened, and spoke, and together the two of them became so caught up in the presence of God that a miraculous light shone brighter and brighter all around their humble table. As would happen later on Mt. Alverno, people would remember that day as one when an inexplicable light shone brightly in the distance. In fact, it is even said that some men from Assisi ran to Portiuncula in order to put out a blazing fire, but saw only Francis, Clare, and the others with a beautiful meal placed before them, beside themselves in contemplation of God.

In the life to come, we may imagine the Poverello and Pianticella still together, enjoying each other's company at that humble but elaborate banquet. The image of a sumptuous meal is an appealing metaphor for heaven. Who wouldn't want to sit at that table, even if just for a few minutes!

Long before that meal and holy conversation in Assisi, a Pharisee named Simon invited Jesus to a meal. When Jesus arrived at Simon's house and took his place at the table, Luke says that a woman came in who had a bad reputation in town. She had heard that Jesus was dining with the Pharisee and brought with her an alabaster jar of ointment. As she was waiting behind Jesus, weeping, her tears fell freely on his feet and she wiped them with her hair. Then she covered his feet with kisses and anointed them again. The Pharisee doubted that Jesus could be a true prophet, since he knew that the woman was disreputable and since he allowed her to touch him. But Jesus said to Simon: "I tell you that her sins, many as they are, have been forgiven her, because she has shown such great love. It is someone who is forgiven little who shows little love." And then he said to the woman, "Your sins are forgiven."[134]

This story of Jesus and the woman with the alabaster jar speaks to why we may feel drawn to Francis and Clare. Jesus forgave the woman's sins not because of her *beliefs*, or even because of her repentance (she does not, in fact, repent using any words), but simply because she *loved*. This is very much how Francis and Clare lived. They did not accumulate many beliefs, and they were not famous for their penitence. They were lovers.

There will always be skeptics on the relevance of living a life in the way of Francis and Clare today. Skeptics will argue that the radical nature of their commitments make for a nice story, but not for a plan of life. If we take evolution at face value, people will say, then humankind originated as a species struggling to survive over other species. We are intended to struggle with each other; unconditional charity for strangers is out-of-date. Families and communities and nations must be protected, and this often means that loving all people seems impossible. Francis and Clare's radical love for their neighbor may have once been possible for friars and sisters, but for the rest of us in the secular world, it simply doesn't work.

Voluntary poverty is unrealistic, they will argue. God wants us to have our hearts' desires. Besides, successful economic systems and social structures are built upon the premise that there will be winners and there will be losers. Hard work is justly rewarded.

Skeptics will argue that redefining *family*—so that we develop attachments with a wide range of people, even strangers and the unwanted, as our brothers, sisters, mothers, and fathers—does not work in our world. We need to care for and provide for and protect our families, first and foremost. What helps my family may directly or indirectly hurt others, but that is just the way it is in a fallen world.

Some of those values praised by Jesus in the Sermon on the Mount—meekness, poverty of spirit, peacemaking, purity of heart—were for a past era. Today, we have to look out for ourselves.

We still live in the Dark Ages when we think or live as if we believe these things. If we live today in a golden age of learning and moral enlightenment as compared to the late Middle Ages, we'd better understand that our vice and inhumanity still rival or exceed what was happening in those centuries that we often label as "dark." Our religious sophistication has not cured us of irreligion, which is as common now as it was then. And for all of the progress we have made against superstition, for medicine and education, these enlightenments have not made the famines, misery, ferocity, or ignorance any less.

Francis and Clare turned dark thinking upside down. According to their way of life, winners become losers and losers become winners. This can be done dramatically, as in the example of St. Maximilian Kolbe, who offered to die in a Nazi concentration camp in place of another man because the other man had children to care for. By giving up what little power he had left, Maximilian Kolbe gained everything that matters most. But it happens most often in very subtle, less dramatic, unseen ways. What would happen if Christians were to begin to follow Jesus in some of the ways of Francis and Clare? The world as we know it would change slowly but surely into something resembling the kingdom of God that we yearn for.

In the Sermon on the Mount, Jesus asked us to be perfect. Remove from your mind the images created by others as to what "perfect" means. When we love, we are remembering Christ's love for us, but more important, we are literally re-membering the broken Christ. That's perfect. Much more than recalling what Christ once did, to be the body of Christ is to literally put him back together in that new formation that Jesus hinted about and Francis and Clare remind us of. That's perfect. When we accept that Christ has given us the power to forgive sins—"not seven times, seventy times seven"—we realize that we are called to become like God. That's perfect. When we begin to become who we are supposed to become indwelled by Christ, that is perfect.

His biographers tell us that Francis was profoundly affected by the words "The Word was made flesh" from the beginning of John's Gospel. Francis felt a great tenderness toward the incarnate Christ lying in a stable manger; and he felt passionately driven to make sense out of the responsibility of having the same stuff on his bones and in his heart as Christ had.

Both Francis and Clare lived an incarnational life, seeing themselves as more fully human the more that they became like Christ. They showed God's presence not by argument or even by teaching so much as by the way they embodied it. According to Francis and Clare, the purpose of faith is to follow Christ, and the purpose of following Christ is salvation for others. Salvation is not only for the soul; it is not, in fact, primarily about the soul. Following Christ means saving the world in each situation presented to us: that's the goal of perfection. It means bringing about the kingdom of God, which, as Jesus said, is right here and now. When Francis and Clare burst on the scene at the beginning of the thirteenth century, they were faced with enormous corruption in the Church, war between cities and religions, and malaise from those who had grown tired of what wasn't true about faith. Theirs may remind us of earlier eras, or even our own.

Think back to when Jesus cleared the temple in John's Gospel, chapter two. Worship at that time was based on money (the ability to pay) and the slaughter of animals. John tells us that in the temple Jesus found those who were selling everything from pigeons to oxen. The pigeons were for those with little money and the oxen for those with much. The money-changers were the men who would exchange your Roman coins with images of Caesar on them for currency that was allowed in the temple, without such images. The money-changers of course added a surcharge onto each of those transactions, which were necessary before you could buy your animal for sacrifice in the temple. Jesus came to save his people from religion—this sort of religion. Francis and Clare did the same.

We must continually overcome what happened on the Milvian Bridge in AD 312. It was there and then that the Emperor Constantine saw a vision of a cross in the sky "above the sun"—according to the story he later told to Eusebius of Caesarea—along with the words "Conquer by this." The night after his vision of the cross in the noonday sun, Constantine said that Christ appeared to him in a dream and commanded him to use the Chi-Rho sign, a symbol that features the first two Greek letters of the name Christ, "as a safeguard" in battle. So he outfitted his soldiers with the symbol and they marched on Rome and conquered Constantine's rival, Maxentius, saying that their victory was thanks to the true god of Christianity. Within a few years, Christianity was treated as the favored faith in the empire, and Christians went from a persecuted minority to the state religion within a decade. What had been protected, nurtured, brilliant, and passionate in small communities of committed believers and the catacombs became *official*. What the Christians of antiquity and the Middle Ages believed to have been God's providence and greatest miracle may have, in fact, created a big obstacle to true faith.

Francis and Clare made clear by their lives that being a follower of Christ can sometimes get lost amid the details of being a cultural Christian. Many Christian observers in India eighty years ago thought that they saw St. Francis of Assisi in Mohandas Gandhi. Gandhi never renounced his Hinduism, but he often declared himself a follower of Jesus Christ. There were times during the 1920s and 1930s when Gandhi would arrive to give a lecture and would simply quote from the New Testament, usually from the Sermon on the Mount and the Beatitudes. On one occasion he did this and said: "That is my address to you. Act upon that." A Hindu intellectual of the 1920s said about Gandhi: "What the missionaries have not been able to do in fifty years Gandhi by his life and trial and incarceration has done, namely, he has turned the eyes of India toward the cross."[135]

It is ironic but true that Gandhi may have been a more faithful follower of Christ than many Christians have been. Francis and

Clare return us to the essentials of following the Poor Crucified: Give to the poor; preach good news in your life and with words; worry little about tomorrow; care for creation and its creatures; always show humility; and love your neighbor to the point of sacrificing your life for him. They indeed transformed the darkness of the Middle Ages—and of all ages—by their lives and teachings. What the Crusades could not do, burgeoning papal power did not accomplish, and the threat or promise of hell or heaven would never do, Francis and Clare accomplished with the help of the Holy Spirit. They transformed thousands, and then, over time, millions of lives with their way of life. To live in the spirit of Francis and Clare today is to model Christ in ways that will cause you to be dismissed as a fool, forgotten like the poor, reviled for your optimism, and yet, somehow, remain enormously attractive to the rest of the world who are seeking peace and meaning. Perhaps that is the sort of revolution we need today.

CAST OF CHARACTERS

(by order of their appearance in the book)

Clare of Assisi called herself Francis's *pianticella*, or "little plant," who grew to show God's beauty and provide sustenance for the movement he started. By all accounts, she was a woman of great physical beauty and charm. The document known to history as Clare's *Acts*, written to support her canonization, mentions several marriage proposals. She left domestic life behind at the age of eighteen to become the first woman to follow Francis and was the founder of the Second Order of Franciscans, the Poor Clares. She was a woman of wisdom, sensitivity, and strength. She died on August 11, 1253.

Francis of Assisi called himself the *Poverello*, "little poor man," who unwittingly started a massive movement toward Gospel living, receiving thousands of men and women in the first decade alone, following his own conversion from a life of youthful luxury and uselessness. He died on October 4, 1226.

And the first three to join Francis…

Bernard of Quintavalle remained a lay brother (not a priest), as did all but one of the first twelve followers of Francis. Also like many of the first followers, Bernard came from a prominent and wealthy family in Assisi and was the first person to become a full-time companion of Francis. Tradition holds that this happened on April 16, 1209, when Francis, Bernard, and Peter Catani opened the Scriptures together. He later recruited the first friars in Bologna, in 1211. Bernard died in the early 1240s in Assisi.

Peter Catani joined Francis and Bernard to open the Gospels together at the home of the bishop of Assisi on April 16, 1209. They read Matthew 19:21, Luke 9:3, and Matthew 16:24 in turn, and decided then and there that those words of Christ to the first disciples would also be their rule of life. A well-educated man, Peter was appointed the first minister-general of the Friars Minor in the fall of 1220, when Francis resigned his leadership in the Order. Peter died only a year later, in 1221, at the Portiuncula, where he is also buried.

Giles left the city of Assisi from the east gate that leads down to San Damiano one week after Bernard and Peter had joined Francis, seeking to join him, too. When Francis met Giles on the road, he led him down to the plain to the chapel at Portiuncula and declared him the fourth brother. One of the most legendary and important of the first friars, he traveled the world on early missions, sought martyrdom during the Crusades, as did Francis, and was with Francis when he died. After Francis's death, Giles was a leader among those who deplored the relaxations of the original ideals. He was visited by popes, cardinals, and Bonaventure, and died an old man in 1262 in Assisi's neighboring town of Perugia, where Francis had assigned him and where Giles lived much of his life.

The three known as "the three companions," and others…

Leo was, with Angelo, the closest friend of Francis among the early friars. He was ordained a priest at some early point in the history of the movement, and seems to have become Francis's confessor, traveling with him all over Italy and listening to both his teachings and his troubles. Leo was present at the saint's death, and along with Angelo (and Juniper), was also present at the death of Clare. Leo and Angelo form a vital bridge between the first, best, and most difficult moments of the early Franciscan movement. He died an old man in 1271, and his burial place in the Basilica of St. Francis may be seen today in the crypt below the Lower Church.

Rufinus was a cousin of Clare and called a saint by Francis himself. With Leo and Angelo Tancredi, he joined Francis in 1210, one year after the first disciples. He was with Francis during the important early days in the caves of the Carceri when the friars were spending time each day caring for lepers. And he was with Francis on Mt. Alverno when Francis received the stigmata. There are many stories of Rufinus's having dark visions and temptations from the devil, sometimes aimed at getting him to believe that Francis himself was evil, and Francis was known to counsel Rufinus through these trials. He lived to be very old, dying later than all of the other, original twelve, probably in about 1280. He is also buried in the Basilica of St. Francis.

Angelo Tancredi was a knight before joining Francis, and his bearing always remained noble, despite voluntary poverty. He was the fortunate friar to accompany Francis on the walk that became the first sermon to the birds. He kept vigil at Clare's deathbed and testified at her canonization hearings. Angelo died in 1258 and is the third friar to be buried in the crypt of the basilica. Some scholars have found evidence to suggest that Angelo and Francis may have been biological brothers.

Elias was two years older than Francis. He grew up in and around Assisi and knew Francis from their childhood. A shadow hangs over Elias, as he appears to have had ulterior motives for sanctity from early on. He enjoyed power but lacked the creativity that marked most of the other early followers. He became minister-general after Peter Catani, but his rule was controversial. He was seen as despotic to some, even essentially evil, especially to those who rejected any changes made to Francis's original intentions. Pope Gregory IX dismissed Elias in 1239, and one year later, Elias joined Emperor Frederick II, a violent enemy of the Catholic Church, as an advisor. After a decade of serving Frederick II (whose mercenaries were famously repelled by Clare in their attempt to besiege San Damiano), Elias repented his sins to a priest and the excommunication placed on him was lifted. He died in 1253.

Juniper was a close friend of Clare's, and was among those present at her death. He was a terrific fool, and one of the strictest imitators of the life of Christ that the world has ever seen. Francis of Assisi praised him, believed that he probably possessed the greatest degree of self-knowledge of any of the brothers, and trusted him with various missions and responsibilities. He died in 1258.

Other important friars and Poor Clares listed alphabetically…

Agnes, Clare's sister, joined her in religious life approximately two weeks after Clare's conversion. Agnes was the second member of what came to be known as the Second Order of Franciscans, the Poor Clares. A decade later, Francis and Clare sent Agnes to Monticelli, near Florence, where she served as abbess for more than thirty years. She died in 1253, only a couple of months after her sister Clare.

Agnes of Prague was Clare's contemporary and also the daughter of the king of Bohemia. With Clare's encouragement, Agnes of Prague refused arranged marriages to both Emperor Frederick II and King Henry III of England in order to become a Poor Clare in the Bohemian capital.

Angelo Clareno entered the Order in the decade after Clare's death and knew brothers Leo and Giles. He became the leader of the Spirituals in 1305 and fought in vain to return the Franciscans to Francis's ideals of poverty, work, simplicity, cheerfulness, and preaching. Paul Sabatier wrote: "With him we see the true Franciscan live again, one of those men who, while desiring to remain the obedient son of the Church, cannot reconcile themselves to permit the dream to slip away from them, the ideal to which they have pledged. They often teeter on the borders of heresy; in their speaking against corrupt priests and unworthy popes there is a bitterness which the sectarians of the sixteenth century never exceeded. They seem to renounce all authority and make final appeal to the inward witness of the Holy Spirit, and yet, Protestants would be mistaken to seek their ancestors among such men. No, these Franciscans desired to die as they lived: in the communion of the Church which they loved."[136] Angelo Clareno wrote a book, *Chronicle of the Seven Tribulations*, and claimed that the problems between Conventuals and Spirituals began very early in Francis's ministry. He died in a remote region of Italy, leading the few remaining Spirituals, in 1337.

Anthony of Padua was born around 1195 and was a priest and monk of St. Augustine before joining the Franciscans in 1220. We know that Anthony was present at the General Chapter of 1221 when Francis presented the second edition of his *Rule*. He was known as a great thinker, a theologian, and one of the early followers to turn to learning more than Francis would have liked. He was canonized by the same Gregory IX who canonized Francis, and even more quickly (only one year after his death in 1231).

Bonaventure never actually met Francis, for he was born just as Francis was dying. Bonaventure became minister-general at a contentious time. He wrote a *Life* of the founder that was intended to unify two competing factions: those who were gladly obedient to the pope and cardinals who modified Francis's *Rule*, and the Spirituals who insisted on the original ideals of poverty and humility even when it meant disobedience to their leaders. Soon after Bonaventure's *Life* of Francis was published, all of the previous biographies of Francis were ordered destroyed. He was known as the "Seraphic Doctor," for his combination of personal holiness and brilliant intellect. Bonaventure died in 1274.

Innocent III, one of the most influential and powerful popes of the Middle Ages, strengthened the role of the bishop of Rome in ways that have continued to today. He was pope from 1198–1216, and gave the first, verbal permission to Francis for his new movement.

John of Parma was minister-general before Bonaventure, from 1247–1257. He was minister-general of the Order at the time of Clare's death. John was sympathetic to the cause of the Spirituals and eased restrictions that had been placed on them. He was also an admirer of the teachings of Joachim of Fiore and was tried for heresy related to those teachings after he resigned as minister-general. He was eventually acquitted and retired to a hermitage in Greccio.

John XXII was the pope who effectively brought a swift end to what is called the Spiritual–Conventual controversy, or the fight between those who separated from the Franciscan Order in an attempt to purify it and live according to Francis's original precepts and those who remained within the Order, living according to papal guidelines for it. John called the Spiritual leaders before his court and demanded that they submit to papal authority. "Great is poverty, but greater is obedience," he famously told them. John died in 1334.

Ortolana was the devout mother of Clare who later joined her at San Damiano, becoming a cloistered Poor Clare after the death of her husband. Ortolana died before Clare, but her remains were later buried in the Basilica of St. Clare in Assisi.

Salimbene of Parma wrote "the most remarkable autobiography of the Middle Ages," according to medievalist G. G. Coulton. He was born in 1221 and joined the Franciscans in 1238. He traveled widely in Italy and France and wrote about the corrupt state of the Church in the thirteenth century as well as about the ways that the Friars Minor were changing things for the better.

Cardinal Ugolino (later Pope Gregory IX) took his papal name upon election as an honor to the great reforming pope before him, Gregory VII (1073–1085).[137] As Cardinal Ugolino, appointed in 1217 by Pope Innocent III's successor, Honorius III, to oversee Francis's enthusiastic young movement, he later became pope just before Francis's death, oversaw his canonization, and brought great changes to his Order.

APPENDIX

CHRONOLOGY AND CALENDAR OF IMPORTANT REMEMBRANCES

These dates are taken from a variety of sources, including Raphael Brown's standard edition of *The Little Flowers*, as well as Brown's second appendix to the second English language edition of Omer Englebert's *Saint Francis of Assisi: A Biography*,[138] and various other studies. Dates without days, and even some of those with days, are best estimates only.

CHRONOLOGICAL OUTLINE OF THE EARLY FRANCISCAN MOVEMENT

1181 Francesco Bernardone is born in Assisi. In the absence of his father, Pietro (Peter), his mother gives him the name Giovanni, or John, which is later changed by his father to Francesco, or Francis.

1194 Chiara Favarone is born in Assisi. Her mother, Ortolana, named her Chiara, or Clare, meaning "clear" or "illumined one."

1206 Francis is twenty-four when his conversion begins in earnest. He renounces his earthly father in front of the bishop. Bonaventure writes in his *Life of St. Francis* that Francis's conversion began twenty years before his death (in October 1226). Pope Benedict XVI paid tribute to the eighth centenary of the conversion of Francis in an August 2006 letter written to the Bishop of Assisi.[139]

1209 (February 24) God reveals the way of life to Francis through verses read during Mass from Matthew, chapter ten: "As you go, proclaim that the kingdom of Heaven is close at hand. Cure the sick, raise the dead, cleanse those suffering from virulent skin-diseases, drive out devils. . . . Provide yourselves with no gold or silver, not even with coppers for your purses, with no haversack for the journey or spare tunic or footwear or a staff, for the labourer deserves his keep."

—— (April 16) Bernard of Quintavalle and Peter Catani become the first and second people to formally join Francis. The movement is founded. Soon afterwards, the three of them settle in the abandoned church of St. Mary of the Angels, known as Portiuncula, or "little place."

—— (April 23) Giles becomes the third person to formally join Francis. Soon afterwards, Francis and Giles travel to the Marches of Ancona region of Italy, which would later become identified with the friars who resisted changes to the Order. By the end of the year, Francis and eleven followers walk to Rome to try to see the pope.

1210 Clare hears Francis preach at the Cathedral of San Rufinus in Assisi. Her conversion begins in earnest.

1212 (March 18) Clare shows her renunciation of worldly affairs to the bishop and townspeople of Assisi during the San Rufinus Palm Sunday service. The following evening, she formally joins Francis in his movement, taking the habit as the first sister friar.

1216 (October) A letter of Bishop Jacques of Vitry indicates that there are many communities of "Lesser Brothers" and "Lesser Sisters" in Italy living "according to the form of the primitive Church, about whom it was written: 'The community of believers were of one heart and one mind.'"[140]

1217 or **18** Francis loses control of his Order, abdicates the leadership role, and appoints Peter Catani the first minister-general. Francis struggles to get his friars to adhere to his original values.

1219 A General Chapter of the Order is held at Portiuncula. Five thousand friars attend, signaling the rapid growth of the first decade.

1221 (March 10) Peter Catani dies while Francis is away, and Brother Elias is elected the second minister-general.

1221–1226 Brother Elias is minister-general. Francis calls him his "mother."

1223 (November 29) Pope Honorius III gives the first written papal approval of a *Rule* of Francis.

—— (December 24) Francis creates the first live Nativity while staying at Greccio.

1224 (September 14) Francis receives the stigmata on the Feast of the Holy Cross on Mt. Alverno.

1225 (Spring) Francis composes his hymn, *Canticle of the Creatures*.

1226 (October 3) **Francis dies and is reborn to heaven.**

1227 (March 19) Cardinal Hugolino is elected pope and takes the name Gregory IX.

1228 (July 16) Pope Gregory IX canonizes St. Francis of Assisi.

1229 (February 25) Thomas of Celano presents the first biography of Francis to the pope.

1230 (May 25) The relics of Francis are brought to the Lower Church of the new basilica in Assisi, constructed with walls seven feet thick by design of Brother Elias in order to safeguard the body from intruders. Elias conceals the burial of the body in a wall of solid rock.

1232 Brother Elias begins his reign as minister-general of the Order. He will be dismissed finally by Pope Gregory IX seven years later.

1240 (September) Clare confronts the Saracen mercenaries hired by Emperor Frederick II as they attempt to attack San Damiano.

1253 (August 9) Pope Innocent IV visits Clare on her deathbed and Clare kisses the papal bull, *Solet annuere*, a final approval of her *Rule*.

——— (August 11) **Clare dies and is reborn to heaven.**

1255 (September 26) Pope Alexander IV canonizes St. Clare of Assisi.

——— Thomas of Celano writes the first biography of Clare.

1257 Bonaventure, the Seraphic Doctor, is elected minister-general of the Franciscan order at the age of thirty-six.

1266 All Franciscans are ordered to destroy Thomas of Celano's two biographies of St. Francis.

1288 Former Franciscan minister-general Girolamo da Ascoli Piceno is elected the first Franciscan pope, Nicholas IV.

1318 (May 7) Four friars, known as "Spirituals," are burned at the stake in Marseilles at the urging of their minister-general and Pope John XXII.

1318 The *Mirror of Perfection*, written by Brother Leo and others, is written.

1320s *The Little Flowers* (*Fioretti* in Italian) is compiled by Brother Ugolino and other members of the Spirituals.

Calendar of Important Remembrances

For those who may want to remember these important early Franciscan events in their cycle of daily prayer and worship, what follows is organized by calendar (month/day).

February 24 (1209)   God reveals the way of life to Francis through verses read during Mass from Matthew, chapter ten: "As you go, proclaim that the kingdom of Heaven is close at hand. Cure the sick, raise the dead, cleanse those suffering from virulent skin-diseases, drive out devils. . . . Provide yourselves with no gold or silver, not even with coppers for your purses, with no haversack for the journey or spare tunic or footwear or a staff, for the labourer deserves his keep."

March 18 (1212)   Clare formally joins Francis in his movement, taking the habit as the first sister friar.

April 16 (1209)   Bernard of Quintavalle and Peter Catani become the first and second persons to formally join Francis.

April 23 (1209)   Giles becomes the third person to formally join Francis.

May 25 (1230)   The relics of Francis are brought to the Lower Church of the new basilica in Assisi, constructed with seven-foot-thick walls by design of Brother Elias in order to safeguard the body from intruders. Elias also conceals the burial of the body in a wall of solid rock.

July 16 (1228)   Pope Gregory IX canonizes St. Francis of Assisi.

August 9 (1253)   Pope Innocent IV visits Clare on her deathbed and finally approves her *Rule*.

August 11 (1253)   **Clare dies and is reborn to heaven.** One hundred fifty monasteries of Poor Clares exist throughout Europe at that time.

September 14 (1224)   Francis receives the stigmata on the Feast of the Holy Cross during a Lenten retreat on Mount Alverno.

September 26 (1255)   Pope Alexander IV canonizes St. Clare of Assisi.

October 3 (1226)   **Francis dies and is reborn to heaven.**

December 24 (1223)   Francis creates the first live Nativity while staying at Greccio.

NOTES

1. Thomas of Celano uses a metaphorical sentence for Francis that explains what I mean by not having to take the hair-shirt description of Clare as fact. He writes in chapter 5 of his *Second Life*: "He wore a religious spirit under his worldly clothing," describing the saint in the midst of conversion.

2. *Francis of Assisi: Early Documents,* vol. 1, ed. Regis J. Armstrong, J. A. Wayne Hellmann, and William J. Short (New York: New City Press, 1999), 579.

3. *The Road to Assisi: The Essential Biography of St. Francis,* ed. Jon M. Sweeney (Brewster, MA: Paraclete, 2014), 81.

4. The authorship of the first *Life of Clare,* dated to 1253–1255, has been debated for centuries. It has variously been attributed to St. Bonaventure and others, but there is still strong evidence to support Thomas of Celano as its author. See *Clare of Assisi: Early Documents*, trans. Regis J. Armstrong (New York: New City Press, 2006), 272–75.

5. Now available as *The Road to Assisi: The Essential Biography of St. Francis* (Brewster, MA: Paraclete Press, 2014).

6. All quotes are taken from the first edition edited by Paul Sabatier (see note below for complete biographical information). These lines appear on the last page of the Sabatier edition, followed by "Done in the most holy place of S. Mary of the Little Portion, and completed this fifth of the Ides of May in the year of Our Lord 1228."

7. Sabatier's *Speculum Perfectionis seu S. Francisci Assisiensis legenda antiquissima* appeared in Paris in 1898. The first English translation appeared that same year, published in London. The title page read: "*S. Francis of Assisi the Mirror of Perfection*, written by Brother Leo of Assisi, edited by Paul Sabatier, translated by Sabastian Evans, published by David Nutt."

8. John Moorman, *A History of the Franciscan Order: From Its Origins to the Year 1517* (Oxford: Clarendon Press, 1968), 295.

9. Ozanam was born into a French family living in Milan, Italy. Initially trained as a lawyer, he became a judge in the French city of Lyons. At age twenty, he and some friends began what became known as The Society of St. Vincent de Paul, a ministry aimed at helping the poor of all faith backgrounds during the Industrial Revolution. The Society was named for a Paris priest who had lived more than two hundred years before Ozanam and had spent a lifetime serving the needs of the poor. Ozanam himself never tired of his youthful zeal to put his words into practice and to live the gospel. The Society soon spread throughout the world and was established in the United States by 1845.

10. Robert H. Hopcke and Paul A. Schwartz, *Little Flowers of Francis of Assisi: A New Translation* (Boston: New Seeds, 2006), xiv–xv.

11. Unless otherwise noted, quotations from medieval sources are the author's own translations.

12. *Dialogues II*, chapters 33–34.

13. Just to name two: St. Wilgefort asked God for (and was granted) a beard in order to disgust her male suitors. Similarly, Catherine of Siena sheared her long, blond hair for the same reasons, wanting to simply spend time in seclusion and prayer.

14. As we have seen in recent years, works of fiction—such as Dan Brown's *The Da Vinci Code*—can greatly influence public opinion about religious history and spiritual thought. This is nothing new, as Kazantzakis was doing the same a generation ago.

15. Nikos Kazantzakis, *Saint Francis*, trans. P. A. Bien (New York: Simon and Schuster, 1962), 21. Kazantzakis refers to Clare's father as Count Scifi, taking his cue from the great French biographer Paul Sabatier, who made the same mistake in his classic life of the saint. Clare's family name was actually Offreduccio.

16. Ibid., 226.

17. Ibid., 228.

18. Kazantzakis was Orthodox, and some bishops of the Orthodox Church in America have also regretted his romantic notions of the

life and faith of St. Francis, but for very different reasons from my own. Responding to a sympathetic letter about Francis written to an Orthodox magazine, the editors recently responded: "For several centuries, various Orthodox intellectuals . . . have succumbed to the lure of a theatrical and romantic Western vision of sanctity largely unknown in the pre-Schism East or West (except as a symptom of spiritual delusion), but perfectly captured in the cultus of Francis of Assisi. . . . He was a fanatic Papist, lived after the separation of the Roman Catholic Church from Orthodoxy, and practiced a romantic and emotional spirituality foreign to genuine Orthodox spiritual traditions." *Orthodox Tradition* 12, no. 2, 41–42.

19. A film version of the life of Francis of Assisi that is more faithful to reality, yet still full of emotion and beauty, is Roberto Rossellini's *The Flowers of St. Francis*: 1950, 87 minutes, cowritten by Roberto Rossellini and Federico Fellini. It was filmed in black and white, in Italian with English subtitles, and is currently available on DVD from The Criterion Collection.

20. Gloria Hutchinson, *Clare of Assisi: The Anchored Soul* (Cincinnati: St. Anthony Messenger Press, 1982), 1. (This is a pamphlet taken from the larger book *Six Ways to Pray from Six Great Saints*, by the same author.)

21. Adrian House, *Francis of Assisi: A Revolutionary Life* (Mahwah, NJ: Hiddenspring, 2001), 135.

22. Murray Bodo, *Clare: A Light in the Garden* (Cincinnati: St. Anthony Messenger Press, 1992), 13.

23. Miguel de Unamuno, *Our Lord Don Quixote*, trans. Anthony Kerrigan (Princeton: Princeton University Press, 1967), 77.

24. The following stories had their origin in Thomas of Celano's *Second Life* of St. Francis. They were curiously excluded from Thomas's *First Life*.

25. Matthew 5:40–41.

26. Quoted in Norman Davies, *Europe: A History* (New York: Oxford University Press, 1998), 279–80.

27. Luke 16:19–20.

28. *The Legend of the Three Companions*, ch. 4.

29. Umberto Eco, *Art and Beauty in the Middle Ages*, trans. Hugh Bredin (New Haven: Yale University Press, 1986), 55.

30. Søren Kierkegaard, *Training in Christianity*, trans. Walter Lowrie (Princeton: Princeton University Press, 1944), 108.

31. Shusaku Endo, *Silence*, trans. William Johnston (Rutland, VT: Tuttle, 1970), 219.

32. Ilia Delio, OSF, *Franciscan Prayer* (Cincinnati: St. Anthony Messenger Press, 2004), 6.

33. The kissing the leper scene is chapter 5 of Thomas of Celano's *Second Life*. This phrase is from chapter 6, at the beginning of the story that is to follow.

34. Translated by Thomas Lentes in "'As far as the eye can see…': Rituals of Gazing in the Late Middle Ages," in *The Mind's Eye: Art and Theological Argument in the Middle Ages*, ed. Jeffrey F. Hamburger and Anne-Marie Bouche (Princeton: Princeton University Press, 2006), 360.

35. Quote from Salimbene taken from G. G. Coulton's *From St. Francis to Dante: Translations from the Chronicle of the Franciscan Salimbene (1221– 88)*, 2nd ed. (Philadelphia: University of Pennsylvania Press, 1972), 297. Slight changes to punctuation and spelling are made throughout in an effort to bring the translations up to date.

36. Ibid., 49.

37. Augustine Thompson, OP, *Cities of God: The Religion of the Italian Communes, 1125–1325* (University Park: Pennsylvania State University Press, 2005), 381. Salimbene joined the Friars Minor in 1238 and traveled widely, writing about what he saw in the Church and in the Franciscan Order.

38. Quoted in Eamon Duffy, *Saints and Sinners: A History of the Popes,* 2nd ed. (New Haven: Yale University Press, 2001), 128.

39. *The Legend of the Three Companions*, ch. 7, 21.

40. G. K. Chesterton, *St. Francis of Assisi* (London: Hodder & Stoughton, 1946), 67–68.

41. *The Mirror of Perfection*, chs. 56–57.

42. Bonaventure, *Life*, ch. 2, 4.

43. *The Legend of the Three Companions*, ch. 6, 17.

44. Bonaventure, *Life*, ch. 2, 3.

45. Thomas of Celano, *First Life*, 98.

46. See Gerald B. Guest, "The Prodigal's Journey: Ideologies of Self and City in the Gothic Cathedral," *Speculum* 81 (2006): 35–75.

47. Luke 2:48–50.

48. *The Rule of St. Benedict*, trans. Anthony C. Meisel and M. L. del Mastro (Garden City, NY: Image Books, 1975), ch. 58, 93, 95.

49. Johannes Jorgensen, *Saint Francis of Assisi*, trans. T. O'Conor Sloane (New York: Longmans, Green, and Company, 1913), 127.

50. *The Little Flowers*, ch. 26.

51. Quoted from Chesterton's essay that began as a review of a devotional book about St. Francis and was then collected into the book *Twelve Types*, and again as *Varied Types*.

52. Moorman, *A History of the Franciscan Order*, 10.

53. Thomas of Celano, *Second Life*, ch. 9.

54. Eve Borsook, *The Companion Guide to Florence* (London: Fontana Books, 1973), 114–15.

55. *The Mirror of Perfection*, ch. 15.

56. David Burr, *The Spiritual Franciscans: From Protest to Persecution in the Century after Saint Francis* (University Park: University of Pennsylvania Press, 2001), 6.

57. *The Mirror of Perfection*, chs. 39 and 41.

58. Unamuno, *Our Lord Don Quixote*, 11.

59. The following descriptions derive, in part, from Augustine Thompson, OP, *Cities of God*, 314–19.

60. 1 Corinthians 11:1.

61. The chapter numbers and Scripture quotations are taken from Paul Sabatier's classic edition of *The Mirror of Perfection*, 1898.

62. Christian Bobin, *The Very Lowly: A Meditation on Francis of Assisi*, trans. Michael H. Kohn (Boston: New Seeds, 2006), 83.

63. Rosalind B. Brooke, *Early Franciscan Government* (Cambridge: Cambridge University Press, 1959), 85.

64. Simone Weil, *Letter to a Priest*, trans. Arthur Wills (New York: G. P. Putnam's Sons, 1954), 36–37.

65. Bernard of Clairvaux, *On the Song of Songs,* vol. 1, trans. Kilian Walsh (Kalamazoo, MI: Cistercian Publications, 1981), 6. The first sentence of the quote is from the Walsh translation; the rest is my own.

66. *The Little Flowers*, xxvii.

67. Thomas of Celano, *Second Life*, ch. 146.

68. Boyd Taylor Coolman, *Knowing God by Experience: The Spiritual Senses in the Theology of William of Auxerre* (Washington, D.C.: Catholic University of America Press, 2004), 9.

69. In keeping with his commitment not to own anything, not to touch money, and yet not to be beholden to any other religious organization, Francis sent a basket of fresh fish to the abbot of the Benedictines once a year as payment of rent.

70. Since Holy Week of 1957, the San Damiano crucifix—which is known throughout the world—has hung over the altar in San Giorgio's Chapel in the Basilica of St. Clare in Assisi. This is the oldest part of the church, apart from the crypt.

71. Thompson, *Cities of God*, 141–42.

72. 1 Timothy 5:5.

73. Chesterton, *St. Francis of Assisi,* 85–6.

74. Jorgensen, *Saint Francis of Assisi*, 340.

75. Thompson, *Cities of God*, 339.

76. Hopcke and Schwartz, *Little Flowers of Francis of Assisi*, 20.

77. Ibid., 22.

78. *The Mirror of Perfection*, ch. 48.

79. Chapter 2, par. 7. All quotes from the writings of Clare are the present author's translations, based on comparisons with several existing translations. The most authoritative resource for the writings of Clare is currently *Clare of Assisi: Early Documents,* rev. ed., trans. Regis J. Armstrong, OFM Cap. (New York: New City Press, 2006). For the sake of easy reference, each quote from the writings of Clare will reference the paragraph of the letter, *Rule*, or *Testament* from Armstrong's edition.

80. Beatrice of Nazareth, in *Mediaeval Netherlands Religious Literature*, trans. E. Colledge (New York: London House and Maxwell, 1965), 27.

81. Jacobus de Voragine, *The Golden Legend: Readings on the Saints*, vol. 2, trans. William Granger Ryan (Princeton: Princeton University Press, 1993), 225–26.

82. But it does help to be pre-Copernican in order to believe these things. Physicist James Trefil wrote in *The Dark Side of the Universe*: "It's hard to imagine a more gloomy ending to the Copernican odyssey, particularly if you want to believe in your heart of hearts that the earth and its occupants occupy a special place in the universe." The sixteenth-century English poet and preacher John Donne said: "Man, now displaced from the center of the universe, not only sustained a loss of dignity, purpose and direction, but also he was tragically and psychologically divorced from God, the all-unifying center."

83. Thompson, *Cities of God*, 348–49, 378.

84. These stories would never be published as a children's book today; they are best read by older readers. They read like additions to *The Little Flowers,* which was obviously the intention of the anonymous creator. *The Chronicles of Brother Wolf written by Tertius*, illustrated by Sylvia Green (London: A. R. Mowbray and Company, 1939 and 1952), 99, 102. I have modernized the language of the text only slightly.

85. These tales of birds come from Thomas of Celano, *Second Life,* chs. 126, 127, 129. Some are shared in Bonaventure's *Life*.

86. Luke 15:3–7. The quotation of John the Baptist comes from John 1:29.

87. Bonaventure, *Life*, ch. 8, 6.

88. Jacques Dalarun, "Francis and Clare: Differing Perspectives on Gender and Power," *Franciscan Studies* 63 (2005): 16.

89. See *The Assisi Compilation*, ch. 110.

90. Quotes from this text are all taken from *Clare of Assisi: Early Documents* (New York: New City Press, 2006), 259.

91. Thomas of Celano, *Second Life*, ch. 151.

92. Isaiah 6:1–6.

93. Katherine H. Tachau, "Seeing as Action and Passion in the Thirteenth and Fourteenth Centuries," in *The Mind's Eye*, 336–59.

94. Translation by Katherine H. Tachau, "Seeing as Action and Passion in the Thirteenth and Fourteenth Centuries," in *The Mind's Eye*, 343.

95. *The Legend of the Three Companions*, ch. 17, 69.

96. The story of Padre Pio is a fascinating one. His superiors were consistently suspicious of his wounds, questioning their validity for most of the friar's life, but there is no doubt that the mystery of the inexplicable surrounded Padre Pio all his life, making him perhaps the most popular Catholic religious figure of the last century.

97. *Francis of Assisi: Early Documents,* vol. 2, ed. Regis J. Armstrong, J. A. Wayne Hellmann, and William J. Short (New York: New City Press, 2000), 489–90.

98. *13th Century Chronicles*, trans. Placid Herman (Chicago: Franciscan Herald Press, 1961), 57.

99. *The Legend of the Three Companions*, ch. 17.

100. Jacques Dalarun, "The Great Secret of Francis," in *The Stigmata of Francis of Assisi: New Studies, New Perspectives* (St. Bonaventure, NY: Franciscan Institute Publications, 2006), 19.

101. Thomas of Celano, *Second Life*, ch. 154.

102. Bonaventure, as quoted in Moorman, *A History of the Franciscan Order*, 260.

103. Thomas of Celano, *Life of Clare*, 30.

104. Barbara Newman, "Love's Arrows: Christ as Cupid in Late Medieval Art and Devotion," in *The Mind's Eye*, 263–86.

105. E. B. Pusey translation.

106. Teresa of Avila, *The Complete Works of St. Teresa of Avila,* vol. 1, trans. E. Allison Peers (London: Sheed & Ward, 1946), 192–93.

107. Quoted in Newman, "Love's Arrows," in *The Mind's Eye*, 271.

108. Ilia Delio, OSF, *Franciscan Prayer* (Cincinnati, OH: St. Anthony Messenger Press, 2004), 136.

109. *The Mirror of Perfection*, tale 100.

110. Ibid., tale 101.

111. Ibid., tale 123.

112. From The Book of Common Prayer 1979, Episcopal Church USA.

113. When Francis was faced with the horrific effects of leprosy, his story also reminds us of the Buddha's, who saw death and suffering for the first time as a young man and learned there and then that the world was not as his father had led him to believe. But, unlike Buddha, but

like a true follower of Christ, Francis returned to face the leprosy-afflicted beggar, and he kissed him.

114. Paul Sabatier, *Life of St. Francis of Assisi*, trans. Louise Seymour Houghton (New York: Charles Scribner's Sons, 1938), xxxiii. In quoting from Sabatier's biography, I use the same principles in modifying the translation as I used in *The Road to Assisi: The Essential Biography of St. Francis*; see 171–72 of the latter work.

115. Sabatier, *Life of St. Francis of Assisi*, 275.

116. Heiko A. Oberman, *Luther: Man Between God and the Devil* (New Haven, CT: Yale University Press, 2006), 26.

117. Harold Elsdale Goad, *Franciscan Italy* (New York: Methuen and Company, 1926), 70.

118. Thompson, *Cities of God*, 409–11.

119. Translation of Johannes Jorgensen, *St. Francis of Assisi*, 380.

120. Translation is my own, modifying slightly that of David Burr, *The Spiritual Franciscans*, 36–37.

121. Thomas of Celano, *First Life*, 98, 109 (these are the sections of the work as divided by scholars).

122. But some commentators have argued the reverse: that Salimbene betrayed Elias by becoming such a critical and one-sided detractor, despite all the good that Elias obviously did for him as a young man. See Brooke, *Early Franciscan Government*, 45–55.

123. John Moorman, *A History of the Franciscan Order*, 57.

124. *Saint Francis of Assisi: The Legends and Lauds*, ed. Otto Karrer (New York: Sheed & Ward, 1948), 152.

125. Unamuno, *Our Lord Don Quixote*, 14.

126. Paul Sabatier, *The Road to Assisi*, 28.

127. These are the often-quoted opening lines from chapter 42.

128. From The Book of Common Prayer 1979, Episcopal Church USA.

129. An image of this painting can be seen on The National Gallery's Web site:

http://www.nga.gov/cgi-bin/pinfo?Object=41425+0+none.

130. *Paradiso*, xxxiii, trans. Dorothy L. Sayers.

131. Moorman, *A History of the Franciscan Order*, 185.

132. *Francis of Assisi: Early Documents,* vol. 1, ed. Regis J. Armstrong et al., 86.

133. *Angelo Clareno: A Chronicle or History of the Seven Tribulations of the Order of Brothers Minor,* trans. David Burr and Emmett Randolph Daniel (St. Bonaventure, NY: Franciscan Institute Publications, 2005), 157.

134. Luke 7:36–38, 47–48.

135. Quoted in the Methodist missionary E. Stanley Jones's *The Christ of the Indian Road* (New York: Abingdon Press, 1925), 78. The Anglican missionary to India C. F. Andrews also compared Gandhi to St. Francis in several places in his books, including *Mahatma Gandhi's Ideas Including Selections from His Writings* (London: George Allen & Unwin, 1929).

136. Sabatier, *Life of St. Francis of Assisi,* 1938, 410–11.

137. Pope Gregory VIII—Gregory IX's immediate predecessor in name— was pope for only two months in 1187.

138. Omer Englebert, *Saint Francis of Assisi: A Biography,* 2nd English ed., trans. Eve Marie Cooper, revised and augmented by Ignatius Brady, OFM, and Raphael Brown (Chicago: Franciscan Herald Press, 1965).

139. The letter was read to the attendees of a conference in Assisi. Robert Mickens, "Pope re-evaluates 'spirit of Assisi,'" *The Tablet,* September 9, 2006, 30.

140. *Francis of Assisi: Early Documents,* vol. 1, ed. Regis J. Armstrong et al., 579.

ACKNOWLEDGMENTS

Many thanks go to the people who have read and commented on the manuscript, as well as to my insightful editors, Patricia Nakamura and Robert J. Edmonson. Many thanks, too, to Marek Czarnecki, the talented Connecticut-based iconographer who has graciously granted permission to reproduce his icon of Francis and Clare in this book. All of the other illustrations are reproductions of the photographic images of Giotto paintings in Basil de Selincourt's classic, *Giotto* (London and New York, 1905).

Two of my sources deserve special mention. Each has been recently published and, as any reader of the notes portion of the present work will testify, I am indebted to both of them for many of my ideas. These are *The Mind's Eye: Art and Theological Argument in the Middle Ages*, edited by Jeffrey F. Hamburger and Anne-Marie Bouche, from Princeton University Press, 2006, and Augustine Thompson's masterful *Cities of God: The Religion of the Italian Communes, 1125-1325*, published in 2005 by Penn State Press.

I dedicate this book to Christina Brannock, who has taught me much that is in here. Nevertheless, to paraphrase G. K. Chesterton's introductory note to his classic book on Thomas Aquinas, the aim of the present work will be achieved if it leads those who have reflected a little on the lives of Francis and Clare of Assisi to now read more about them in better books.

INDEX OF NAMES, SUBJECTS, AND SCRIPTURES

About Paraclete Press

Who We Are

Paraclete Press is a publisher of books, recordings, and DVDs on Christian spirituality. Our publishing represents a full expression of Christian belief and practice—from Catholic to Evangelical, from Protestant to Orthodox. We are the publishing arm of the Community of Jesus, an ecumenical monastic community in the Benedictine tradition. As such, we are uniquely positioned in the marketplace without connection to a large corporation and with informal relationships to many branches and denominations of faith.

What We Are Doing

BOOKS Paraclete publishes books that show the richness and depth of what it means to be Christian. Although Benedictine spirituality is at the heart of all that we do, we publish books that reflect the Christian experience across many cultures, time periods, and houses of worship. We publish books that nourish the vibrant life of the church and its people—books about spiritual practice, formation, history, ideas, and customs.

We have several different series, including the best-selling Paraclete Essentials and Paraclete Giants series of classic texts in contemporary English; Voices from the Monastery—men and women monastics writing about living a spiritual life today; award-winning poetry; best-selling gift books for children on the occasions of baptism and first communion; and the Active Prayer Series that brings creativity and liveliness to any life of prayer.

RECORDINGS From Gregorian chant to contemporary American choral works, our music recordings celebrate sacred choral music through the centuries. Paraclete distributes the recordings of the internationally acclaimed choir Gloriæ Dei Cantores, praised for their "rapt and fathomless spiritual intensity" by *American Record Guide*, and the Gloriæ Dei Cantores Schola, which specializes in the study and performance of Gregorian chant. Paraclete is also the exclusive North American distributor of the recordings of the Monastic Choir of St. Peter's Abbey in Solesmes, France, long considered to be a leading authority on Gregorian chant.

VIDEOS Our videos offer spiritual help, healing, and biblical guidance for life issues: grief and loss, marriage, forgiveness, anger management, facing death, and spiritual formation.

Learn more about us at our Web site: www.paracletepress.com, or call us toll-free at 1-800-451-5006.

SCAN TO READ MORE

Also by Jon M. Sweeney

The St. Francis Prayer Book
A Guide to Deepen Your Spiritual Life

144 pages | ISBN: 978-1-55725-352-1 | $15.99, paperback

This warm-hearted little book is a window into the soul of St. Francis, one of the most passionate and inspiring followers of Jesus. "Prayer was to Francis as play is to a child—natural, easy, creative, and joyful," author Jon Sweeney tells us.

With this guide, you will:

• Pray the words that Francis taught his spiritual brothers and sisters to pray.

• Explore Francis's time and place and feel the joy and earnestness of the first Franciscans.

• Experience how it is possible to live a contemplative and active life, at the same time.

Also by Jon M. Sweeney

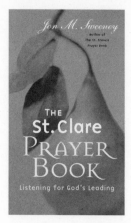

The St. Clare Prayer Book
Listening for God's Leading
192 pages | ISBN: 978-1-55725-513-6 | $16.99, paperback

Refresh your prayer life and deepen your relationship with God by exploring seven themes from the life of St. Clare:

- Embracing Christ

- Purity

- Walking the path of conversion

- Listening with the heart

- Adoring Christ

- True discipleship

- Redefining family

Available from most booksellers or through Paraclete Press:
www.paracletepress.com; 1-800-451-5006
Try your local bookstore first.